I0748467

MARK TWAIN

Mark Twain, 1901. Courtesy of The Mark Twain Project, The Bancroft Library.

MARK TWAIN

Protagonist for the Popular Culture

Marlene Boyd Vallin

Great American Orators, Number 18

Bernard K. Duffy and Halford R. Ryan,
Series Advisers

Greenwood Press
Westport, Connecticut • London

Library of Congress Cataloging-in-Publication Data

Vallin, Marlene Boyd.
Mark Twain : protagonist for the popular culture / Marlene Boyd Vallin.
p. cm.—(Great American orators, ISSN 0898-8277 ; no. 18)
Includes bibliographical references and index.
ISBN 0-313-27353-7 (alk. paper)
1. Twain, Mark, 1835-1910—Criticism and interpretation.
2. Speeches, addresses, etc., American—History and criticism.
3. Speeches, addresses, etc., American. 4. United States—Popular culture. 5. Oratory—United States. I. Title. II. Series.
PS1338.V35 1992
818'.409—dc20 92-17861

British Library Cataloguing in Publication Data is available.

Library of Congress Catalog Card Number: 92-17861
ISBN: 0-313-27353-7
ISSN: 0898-8277

First published in 1992

Greenwood Press, 88 Post Road West, Westport, CT 06881
An imprint of Greenwood Publishing Group, Inc.

Printed in the United States of America

The paper used in this book complies with the Permanent Paper Standard issued by the National Information Standards Organization (Z39.48-1984).

10 9 8 7 6 5 4 3 2 1

Copyright Acknowledgment

The author and publisher are grateful to HarperCollins for allowing the reprinting of "On Speech-Making Reform," "On Foreign Critics," and "Advice to Youth," taken from Samuel L. Clemens, *Mark Twain's Speeches* (New York: Harper and Brothers, 1923).

To my family

Contents

Series Foreword

The idea for a series of books on great American orators grew out of the recognition that there is a paucity of book-length studies on individual orators and their speeches. Apart from a few notable exceptions, the study of American public address has been pursued in scores of articles published in professional journals. As helpful as these studies have been, none has or can provide a complete analysis of a speaker's rhetoric. Book-length studies, such as those in this series, will help fill the void that has existed in the study of American public address and its related disciplines of politics and history, theology and sociology, communication and law. In a book, the critic can explicate a broader range of a speaker's persuasive discourse than reasonably could be treated in an article. The comprehensive research and sustained reflection that books require will undoubtedly yield many original and enduring insights concerning the nation's most important voices.

Public address has been a fertile ground for scholarly investigation. No matter how insightful their intellectual forbears, each generation of scholars must reexamine its universe of discourse, while expanding the compass of its researches and redefining its purpose and methods. To avoid intellectual torpor new scholars cannot be content simply to see through the eyes of those who have come before them. We hope that this series of books will stimulate important new understandings of the nature of persuasive discourse and provide additional opportunities for scholarship in the history and criticism of American public address.

This series examines the role of rhetoric in the United States. American speakers shaped the destiny of the colonies, the young republic, and the mature nation. During each stage of the intellectual, political, and religious development of the United States, great orators, standing at the rostrum, on the stump, and in the pulpit, used words and gestures to influence their audiences. Usually striving for the noble, sometimes achieving the base, they urged their fellow citizens toward a more perfect Union. The books in this series chronicle and explain the accomplishments of representative American leaders as orators.

A series of book-length studies on American persuaders honors the role men and women have played in U.S. history. Previously, if one desired to assess the impact of a speaker or a speech upon history, the path was, at best, not well marked and, at worst, littered with obstacles. To be sure, one might turn to biographies and general histories to learn about an orator, but for the public address scholar these sources often prove unhelpful. Rhetorical topics, such as speech invention, style, delivery, organizational strategies, and persuasive effect, are often treated in passing, if mentioned at all. Authoritative speech texts are often difficult to locate, and the problem of textual accuracy is frequently encountered. This is especially true for those figures who spoke one or two hundred years ago or for those whose persuasive role, though significant, was secondary to other leading lights of the age.

Each book in this series is organized to meet the needs of scholars and students of the history and criticism of American public address. Part I is a critical analysis of the orator and his or her speeches. Within the format of a case study, one may expect considerable latitude. For instance, in a given chapter an author might explicate a single speech or a group of related speeches, or examine orations that comprise a genre of rhetoric such as forensic speaking. But the critic's focus remains on the rhetorical considerations of speaker, speech, occasion, and effect. Part II contains the texts of important addresses that are discussed in the critical analysis that precedes it. To the extent possible, each author has endeavored to collect authoritative speech texts, which have often been found through original research in collections of primary source material. In a few instances, because of the extreme length of a speech, texts have been edited, but the authors have been careful to delete material that is least important to the speech, and these deletions have been held to a minimum.

In each book there is a chronology of major speeches that serves more purposes than may be apparent at first. Pragmatically, it typically lists all of the orator's known speeches and addresses. Places and dates of the speeches are also listed, although this is information that is sometimes difficult to determine precisely. But in a wider sense, the chronology attests to the scope of rhetoric in the United States. Certainly in quantity, if not always in quality, Americans are historically talkers and listeners.

Because of the disparate nature of the speakers examined in the series, there is some latitude in the nature of the bibliographical materials that have been included in each book. But in every instance, authors have carefully described original historical materials and collections and gathered critical studies, biographies and autobiographies, and a variety of secondary sources that bear on the speaker and the oratory. By combining in each book bibliographical materials, speech texts, and critical chapters, this series notes that text and research sources are interwoven in the act of rhetorical criticism.

May the books in this series serve to memorialize the nation's greatest orators.

Bernard K. Duffy
Halford R. Ryan

Foreword

When one conceives of a great American orator, the eighteenth century prompts a Patrick Henry or a John Hancock, the nineteenth century a Daniel Webster or an Abraham Lincoln. Indeed, the mid-eighteenth century is called the golden age of American public address. But speaking continued after the Civil War, and Americans witnessed a subsequent age that was known for its silver-tongued oratory.

Mark Twain was such a nineteenth-century speaker. Yet he is not commonly thought of in company with Henry Ward Beecher, Robert Green Ingersoll, or Booker T. Washington. Part of the problem might be in regard to the genre of Twain's oratory.

Of Aristotle's three genres of speaking, it appears that historians and critics always have preferred two genres—almost to the exclusion of the third kind. Forensic oratory implies momentous judicial cases argued by a Henry, a Webster, and, in the twentieth century, a Clarence Darrow. Deliberative speaking suggests the great legislative triumvirate of Webster, Clay, and Calhoun. But epideictic rhetoric, which includes ceremonial or occasional speaking such as Fourth of July speeches, after-dinner speeches, commencement addresses, funeral orations, and the like, have unexplainably played a lesser role in the pageantry of American public address.

Professor Marlene Vallin revises the rhetorical record in this book on two needed points in the history and criticism of public speech. First, she brings to center stage, a place to which Twain was accustomed in his lifetime, a man and his oratory. Vallin uses contemporary rhetorical principles to illuminate the genius of Twain's nineteenth-century theory and practice. On both accounts, his was no mean feat. Second, Vallin elucidates how epideictic speaking was a ceremonial, yet practical and successful rhetorical genre, especially in the hands of a skilled communicator such as Mark Twain, to shape the values of Twain's era.

Thus, if one does not normally think of Mark Twain as a great American orator, who practiced epideictic speaking productively, then Professor Vallin's book overcomes both misconceptions.

Halford R. Ryan

Preface

This book was written for the express purpose of proving that Mark Twain's public speaking presentations were works of oratory. Although he repeatedly stated that his chief purpose was to teach, critics tended to dismiss these performances as mere entertainment. In actuality, Twain feared being regarded as a buffoon. His apparently artless art was crafted skillfully and meticulously. Although his immediate response to lecturing was for financial reasons, he was enchanted by the communication process. He wrote often about his love for spoken language—that it was superior to print because it had soul. Twain reveled in the social interaction between speaker and audience, practicing his delivery to create an intended response. In his forty years on the platform, he responded creatively to the exigencies of his time.

The study of Twain's oratory is important for several reasons. First, it provides an understanding of the development of Twain's oral style of writing. Twain often used the platform to revise his written work so that its style would resemble that of "flexible talk." Second, it affords a more personal view of nineteenth-century America. The Southerner-turned-Westerner bridged the sections of our nation, unifying the widespread and diverse population. Finally, to study Twain's oratory is to gain a clear impression of what it is to be an American. Twain was the embodiment of the American spirit. Although his topics varied, his message was constant: Americans are superior people because of their love of freedom and their commitment to human rights. Indeed, the study of Twain's oratory is vital for today and all time.

Because this book is the first devoted exclusively to the analysis of Twain's oratory, I chose to fortify its purpose by organizing it in forensic style. The first chapter discusses the proposition that Twain was a great American orator; the second delineates the argument; and the third and fourth present the evidence in the form of critical analyses of selected speeches.

The book is divided into two main parts. Part I has five chapters. It consists of the narrative of this study: Chapter 1 introduces the subject, including the rationale, background information, objective, and organization. Chapter 2 presents a comprehensive appraisal of Twain's platform performances as rhetorical acts. This chapter prepares the reader for greater understanding of Chapters 3 and 4. Chapters 3 and 4 are devoted to the critical analysis of selected presentations. Chapter 3 investigates the rhetorical value of Twain's most successful lectures: The "Sandwich Islands Lecture," his humorous, yet eloquent account of his view of the Hawaiian Islands, on which he reported as a young journalist for the *Alta California*; the "Roughing It Lecture," a vernacular account of his travels in the American West which later became the material for his travel book of the same name; and the "The American Vandal Abroad," Twain's irreverent treatment of the American penchant to visit the Old World, based on his reports from the *Quaker City* tour, which later became the two-volume travel book *The Innocents Abroad*. Chapter 4 explores the rhetorical value of Twain's occasional speeches. The speeches are divided into two categories—after-dinner speeches and other occasional speeches. The first three speeches—"On Speech-Making Reform," "Post-Prandial Oratory," and "Whitefriars Club"—are included in this study chiefly because they demonstrate Twain's interest in the art of public speaking. The other speeches in this collection are some of Twain's most celebrated creations: "The Babies," considered one of Twain's most hilarious after-dinner presentations; "Dinner Speech" on the occasion of Whittier's birthday, characterized as "poor Clemens's hideous mistake"; "Plymouth Rock and the Pilgrims," an example of Twain's anger with the dominant culture; "On Foreign Critics," a brilliant defense of the American culture; "Advice to Youth," a classic example of Twain's satirical humor; "Edmund Burke on Croker and Tammany," an inventive indictment of political corruption; "Remarks" and "Introducing Winston S. Churchill," two shocking attacks on Western imperialism; and "Our Guest" and "Seventieth Birthday Speech," two eloquent ceremonial speeches.

Part II of the book is comprised of reference materials that relate to Part I. Texts of the speeches that were chosen for analysis in Part I are included here. The texts for these speeches come from the most recent collection of Twain's speeches, *Mark Twain Speaking*, edited by Paul Fatout, and published by the University of Iowa Press in 1976. Also included in this part is an annotated chronology of the speaking events in Twain's life. The final segment consists of a bibliographic essay which discusses library collections as well as sources most directly concerned with the subject of the book.

It should be noted here that Twain also enjoyed a reputation as a popular platform reader. His tour with George Washington Cable, from 1884 to 1885, and his world tour, from 1895 to 1896, were reading tours. Except for mention in the chronology, these performances are not included in this study. Twain as an oral interpreter of literature is a separate study.

I would like to express particular appreciation to all the librarians who responded so cooperatively to my calls for assistance, to the curators of collections for sharing their material with me, especially to the staff at the Mark Twain Project at Berkeley for their benevolent service, and to the National Endowment for the Humanities for affording me an opportunity to study there.

I
CRITICAL ANALYSIS

1
Mark Twain: A Great American Orator

> "He is a reference figure for all of us . . . marking the common denominator of what we want to perceive to be the American Character."
>
> —Alan Gribben, *Atlantic Quarterly*

RATIONALE FOR THE STUDY

For more than forty years the renowned author, Mark Twain, gained fame and fortune, nationally and internationally, as a platform performer. He called his public speaking his "alternate career" because it paid him well, but it was much more than that. In truth, it was Twain's platform experiences that transformed him from regional journalist to world celebrity. Through these events he gained a keener sense of communication that contributed to the development of his oral style of writing and his charismatic personality. Speaking to the public, Twain claimed, was his "natural trade . . . teaching"[1] and he never ceased perfecting his apparently artless art.[2] Alan Gribben, in his 1986 article in *American Quarterly* states, "Even after he was established as a leading author, he would analyze oral performance much more consciously and astutely than the craft of writing."[3] Louis Budd, in his 1983 book, *Our Mark Twain*, concludes that Twain's rhetoric was defined more succinctly in his speeches than his writings: "More than his writings, the speeches kept scoffing at ossified piety, dull or plagiarized sermons, biblical fundamentalism, the doltish singing of hymns, and superficial notions of virtue."[4] Also, Budd adds, "His oratorical persona got credit for having a somewhat sharper knowledge of the ladies than did Twain the novelist."[5] Mark

Twain's popularity as a public speaker made him one of the most influential men of the nineteenth century. One English journalist commented that Twain's speeches were "probably read by a larger number of men and women in America than any public document, the President's message not excepted."[6]

From 1867 to 1907, from frontier village to foreign capital, Mark Twain spread his perception of the American experience. From the lecture circuit to the reading platform, to the sundry after-dinner speeches, to the scathing political diatribes, Twain's rhetoric of identification resulted in his emergence as the Representative American. To those who raised Crèvecoeur's famous question—"What then is the American, this new man?"—Twain was the answer. His American was one of the common folk spawned from the freedom of the frontier, accountable to nobody but himself. In a December 22, 1881 speech to members of the dominant culture celebrating their descendance from the Pilgrims, the New England Society of Philadelphia, Twain boldly declared himself champion of the common man, the "true American":

> I am a border ruffian from the state of Missouri. I am a Connecticut Yankee by adoption. I have the morals of Missouri and the culture of Connecticut, and that's the combination that makes the perfect man.[7]

According to Robert Rodney, in *The Art, Humor, and Humanity of Twain*: "Almost inevitably the man's presence, his personality, and his attitudes became, in these people's minds, a prototype of the American character."[8]

Throughout his career, Mark Twain was the self-declared standard-bearer of the rapidly emerging popular culture. Like his fictional hero in *A Connecticut Yankee In King Arthur's Court*, he strove to expose the superficial codes of behavior promoted by the dominant culture—the Victorians. He tended to portray the American Everyman, revealing his sinfulness with self-deprecating humor while assaulting the Establishment's hypocrisy with stinging satire. His professed mission was to promote the common sense values of authenticity and autonomy. As hilarious as his performances were, they were meticulously prepared with that purpose in mind. Twain was very sensitive to being regarded simply as an entertainer. In his autobiography, notebooks, and letters, he consistently referred to himself as a teacher. The humorists which were his contemporaries are no longer remembered, he argues, because they were "mere humorists." "Humor is only a fragrance, a decoration," he explained.[9] He believed that in order for humor to survive, it must be based on serious purpose; it must teach and preach.[10] "I have always preached. . . If the humor came of its own accord and uninvited, I have allowed it a place in my sermon, but I was not writing the sermon for the sake of the humor."[11]

In spite of the enormous impact of his public speaking career on Twain, his work, and his world, there is very little scholarship on the subject. The few books, journal articles, and theses available tend to chronicle his performances, only one seems to attempt to analyze them rhetorically. Frederick J. Antczak's *Thought and Character: The Rhetoric of Democratic Education* posits a very valid argument for the rhetorical value of Twain's oratory by including him in the company of Emerson and William James as public speakers credited with teaching democratic principles to American audiences.[12] There have been two collections of Twain's speeches published; both are presently out of print. The first, *Mark Twain Speeches*, was compiled by Albert Bigelow Paine and was published in 1910, the first posthumous book on Twain, and was reissued in 1923.[13] The second, *Mark Twain Speaking*, was edited by Paul Fatout and published in 1976.[14] Fatout presents the texts of 195 speeches, but warns that "[N]o text can be regarded as authoritative."[15] Twain purposely changed his texts to preserve their effectiveness with individual audiences. Fatout explains that a manuscript might claim to have some reliability, for it represents what Twain intended to say, but "it is no more trustworthy than any other text."[16]

One source of the problem stems from the fact that Mark Twain, although meticulous about the preparation of his presentations, tended to deviate from his text in actual delivery. Twain developed a compelling sense of audience and, therefore, adapted his performances accordingly. He also admitted to having a weak memory, describing himself as someone whose "memory was loaded with anything but blank cartridges."[17] When he discovered that the audience's spontaneous reactions to the memory lapses produced favorable responses, he chose to prepare his talks according to symbols rather than manuscript form.[18] This form of preparation enabled him to do what he thought best for the success of his performances—relate extemporaneously to his listeners.

Another source of the problem of not having copies of Twain's speeches exactly as they were delivered is the result of another facet of Twain's performance strategy. Versions of his manuscripts can be found in newspapers and anthologies, for example, but, according to Fatout, they "usually differ from each other."[19] A reason for this inconsistency is that Twain, furious with the printing of verbatim reports or synopses, deliberately changed his texts. He believed that a "synopsis of a humorous lecture holds up all the jokes, in a crippled condition for the world to remember & so remembering them hate them if ever they hear that lecturer repeat them in solemn & excruciating succession one after the other."[20] Twain contended that a verbatim report of a humorous lecture is not a fair representation, for it "leaves the *soul* out of it, and no more presents that lecture to the reader than a person presents a *man* to you when he ships you a corpse."[21]

According to Twain, "[S]ynopses injure—they do harm, because they travel ahead of the lecturer & give people a despicable opinion of him & his production."[22] Furthermore, he objected to verbatim reports because he believed that his lecture was his private property. Twain urged one reporter to take his valise and let his lecture alone: "I own both of them—I *alone*. Take the valise—it is only worth a hundred dollars—the lecture is worth ten thousand."[23] There was a recording made of the speech he made at a dinner honoring his seventieth birthday, but it was ruined.

Fortunately, Twain made a number of comments about his public performances in his notebooks, letters, and autobiography. He also addressed the subject directly in his speech "On Speech-Making Reform"[24] and in his essay "How to Tell a Story."[25] Other primary source material must come from comments of his contemporaries published in newspapers and magazines. Complete works devoted to discussion of his platform career are very sparse. Bernard DeVoto's book *Mark Twain in Eruption: Hitherto Unpublished Pages about Men and Events*, published in 1922, contains a chapter on Twain's notions about the platform. Paul Fatout's *Mark Twain on the Lecture Circuit*, published in 1960, and Fred W. Lorch's *The Trouble Begins at Eight: Mark Twain's Lecture Tours*, published in 1966, chronicle only one phase of Twain's platform career. Louis J. Budd's *Our Mark Twain: The Making of His Public Personality* offers a little more than intermittent comments on the quality of Twain's public speaking.

This author's work—specifically two articles: "Mark Twain, Platform Artist: A Nineteenth-Century Preview of Twentieth-Century Performance Theory," published in *Text and Performance Quarterly* in 1989,[26] and "'Manner Is Everything': The Secret to Mark Twain's Performing Success," published in the *Journal of Popular Culture* in 1990,[27] seem to be the only specific rhetorical studies of Twain's speaking career.

It is time that Twain be recognized officially as a great American orator. In his celebrated series *The Americans*, the historian Daniel Boorstin reports Twain as "one of the greatest lecturers in all of American history."[28] Frederick Antczak's *Thought and Character*, cited earlier, credits Twain's platform work as a major influence in the spread of democratic education in nineteenth-century America. "Had humor been more respectable in his day," summarizes Charles Wagenknecht, "he might occupy a greater portion of the history of American public address."[29]

BACKGROUND INFORMATION

Mark Twain was born into a world where the sound and sight of public speaking was commonplace. American in the nineteenth century was a young nation earnestly determined to develop and prosper. To spread the spirit of nationalism to its growing population and to those inhabitants who chose to settle in the remote corners of its spreading borders, circuits of public speaking were established. From 1831 to after the Civil War, lyceums, with programs of lectures dedicated to the education of the populace, could be found throughout the country. The remainder of the century witnessed the popularity of the Chautauqua movement with its educational programs. Events of public speaking featuring platform performers, stump speakers, traveling actors, and evangelists functioned as the television of the times. Daniel Boorstin, in *The Americans: The National Experience*, quotes a publication in 1829 which notes that from the thirteenth century B.C. to the third century B.C. "Athens did not produce more than fifty-four distinguished orators and rhetoricians. We have had many more than that number within half a century."[30] America's heroes, such as Stephen Douglas and Daniel Webster, were often inspiring orators. The numerous newspapers of the time devoted much space to covering the programs of popular performers. Thus, Twain's fascination with oral language was not necessarily unique; he was, indeed, a product of his times.

As a rule, the professional speaker in nineteenth-century America was a graduate of one of the many training schools that proliferated during the height of the elocutionary movement. The teachings of the movement, based on the theories of the eighteen-century English scholars Thomas Sheridan, Gilbert Austin, and John Walker and the nineteenth-century conclusions of American Dr. James Rush and Frenchman Francois Delsarte, stressed the supremacy of delivery over all the other canons of classical rhetoric. The focus of effectiveness was on how well the performers used their voices and gestures to express emotion.

The orators whom Twain and his fellow Americans heard were products of this training. Private schools of elocution, such as the School of Practical Rhetoric and Oratory, founded by William Russell and James E. Murdoch in 1844, and Emerson College of Oratory, founded by Charles Wesley Emerson in 1891,[31] became the conventional training sites for would-be platform speakers. Performers trained in the excesses of elocution often reduced the speech act to a theatrical display. Since the dominant culture of nineteenth-century America was Victorian, with its obsession for propriety, prescriptive forms of instruction were *de rigueur*. The elocutionists thrived. Their theories dominated the teaching of public speaking through the second decade of the twentieth century.

Surprisingly, Mark Twain, the self-educated Southerner-turned-Western journalist, came to be considered on of the most popular platform performers in spite of the fact that his performances were in stark contrast to the grandiose displays of his elocution-trained counterparts. Ironically, his appeal was that he violated the conventions of delivery. According to Antczak's study of Twain's style, "This fellow acted nothing like the roaring cultural lions who stalked the platforms of the day—nothing like the powerful John Gough, nor the sensational DeWitt Talmadge, nor the princely Bayard Taylor, nor the thundering, compelling, almost Jovian Henry Ward Beecher."[32]

Even more than his compatriots, Mark Twain loved the sound of the spoken word. He developed an apparent phonographic memory that enabled him to replicate dialects years after hearing them. He once exclaimed: "Lord, there's nothing like a human organ to make words live and throb, and lift the bearer to the full altitudes of their meaning."[33] He was well aware of the differences between the processes of writing and speaking:

> Written things are not for speech; their form is literary; they are stiff, inflexible, and will not lend themselves to happy and effective delivery with the tongue— . . . they have to be limbered up, broken up, colloquialized, and turned into the common forms of unpremeditated talk—otherwise they will bore the house and not entertain it.[34]

As the Representative American, Twain used the platform from 1867 until the end of the century to spread the libertarian philosophy of this unique human being, the American. Consistently and doggedly, he promoted the virtues of authenticity and autonomy, those rationales for living that were derived naturally from the uniquely American frontier experience. The American culture was the only *real* one, according to Twain; the others were hypocritical and predicated on romantic illusion—what he called "humbug." He was the protagonist for the popular culture. He considered the American Victorians, those who copied British Victorianism to an extreme and then pushed to spread their beliefs on all Americans, as his antagonists. He targeted those elitists among them, particularly the Boston Brahmins, who set themselves up as superior to the popular culture simply because their cultural background was derived from their affiliations with the Continent. Armed with a speaking arsenal ranging from the light humor of homespun anecdotes, exaggerated characterizations, and colloquial expressions to the stinging shock of irreverence and biting satire, Twain spread this nationalistic view, what Henry Nash Smith calls "the vernacular perspective,"[35] nationally and internationally. His speaking style symbolized his message. In sharp contrast to the "proper" form for oratory as prescribed by the Victorian elocutionists in their many schools of oratory, which proliferated throughout the country,

Mark Twain usually ambled nonchalantly to the podium, acting like the tenderfoot, new and untrained. In reality, his style of presentation was practiced with steadfast purpose; each apparently artless movement was meticulously contrived. He was a master of his craft and, hence, molded the minds of all who listened. During his forty years as a popular public speaker, Twain's public persona, his ethos, developed into the embodiment of the American nationalistic spirit.

Mark Twain made a major contribution to the intellectual life of nineteenth-century America as a democratic educator. The intent of his performances was to spread simple, yet fundamental values aimed to enrich humankind. According to a contemporary, "[H]e has taught unobtrusively, but nonetheless powerfully, the virtues of common sense and honest manliness. If it comes to a choice, these are better than refinement."[36] Through his ethos Twain taught the rewards of self-improvement. Twain's commonsense message, presented in what he called "flexible" talk, spread the vernacular in such a way as to effect the development of American English. According to Antczak, "[t]he language in which Twain communicates his commonsense values 'dates' better than the language of perhaps any other nineteenth-century American orator."[37]

Twain's greatest influence was on the spiritual life of his times. From the platform he conducted his rebellion against the moral hollowness of the dominant culture. He declared war on hypocrisy and vigorously petitioned for the truth. Twain proclaimed himself as liar, but this label was part of his rhetorical strategy. According to Budd, he "used them [lies] so cunningly as to end up with a monumental reputation for bringing out the painful truth through misstatement that nevertheless took dead aim at reality."[38] He reached out to the simple, the ignorant, and to the good-hearted through identification, making them feel better about themselves. He brought optimism to those living bleak lives, brightening their days with his humor. Justly called the "Moralist of the Main," Twain was a humanitarian; his call for justice and freedom for all was constant. Twain was the embodiment of the democratic spirit. Together, he and his listeners celebrated the joy of self-discovery. Each needed the other, and each benefitted from the other. American society as a whole benefitted from Mark Twain.

Mark Twain's life touched on many famous episodes in American history: slavery in the Southern border states, life on the Mississippi, sectionalism, the settlement of the West, the Civil War, Reconstruction, the rise of the common man, the Industrial Revolution, and the Gilded Age. He contributed to the political life of his times by helping to unify the regions through his persona and his philosophy. According to Alan Gribben: "He bridged the West by vanquishing the codes of the East."[39] As an active member of the lyceum movement, Twain helped spread democratic principles to the outreaches of the nation. Nineteenth-century America witnessed not only rapidly moving population but also great population change. After the Anglo-Saxon pioneers other ethnic groups immigrated, bringing with them different customs, languages, culture patterns, and literary backgrounds. If this country was to survive both the language and thinking of this heterogeneous population needed to be unified. Mark Twain, public speaker, not only contributed to that unification; he also deserves much of the credit for popularizing American principles abroad. Mark Twain helped the United States gain respect.

OBJECTIVE OF THE BOOK

It should be evident by now that the study of Twain's speeches has much rhetorical value. From lecture to diatribe, Twain responded to the most pressing exigencies of the times: the rise of the common man, the need to unify Americans, the constraints of Victorianism, the need for public education, the need to purge the United States of foreign influence and standards, the need to acknowledge American English, and the need to show the world that we are a separate and proud people.

Twain's platform performances hold lessons for everyone. As Louis Budd concludes in *Our Mark Twain*, "Perhaps the current generations have little to learn from his more visceral attack on prim nineteenth-century taboos. But hypocrisy, vapid routine, insincerity, and official deceit always make a comeback, and we must keep Mark Twain alive to help us, even against ourselves."[40]

Therefore, the aim of this work is to demonstrate that Mark Twain was a great American orator. This first chapter has presented the case for my proposition. The following chapters will present the argument and the evidence.

2
Rhetorical Appraisal

> "The orator must above all things devote his attention to the formulation of moral character and must acquire a complete knowledge of all that is just and honorable. For without this knowledge no one can be either a good man or skilled in speaking."
> —Quintilian

According to the noted historian Daniel J. Boorstin in his definitive volume *The Americans: The National Experience* and *The History of Public Speaking in America*, Mark Twain was one of the greatest public speakers in American history. And yet the hundreds of Twain's oral creations, that spread the American national spirit worldwide, have generated little scholarly interest. Too readily Twain's performances seemed to have been dismissed as mere entertainment. However, that evaluation is superficial. According to Wayne Booth, in his article titled "The Rhetorical Stance," the entertainer's stance is overly concerned with performance; the speaker with a rhetorical stance focuses on effecting the message to the audience.[1] Mark Twain's stance was rhetorical; his platform presentations were clearly rhetorical acts. His meticulous and relentless attention to every detail of his performances he considered "my duty to my audience."[2] In 1871 he wrote to his wife about performing effectiveness: "Livy darling, the same old practising [*sic*] on audiences still goes on—the same old feeling of pulses and altering manner to suit the symptoms."[3]

Throughout his career, Twain proclaimed that his works had a serious intent—to teach. He commented in one of his notebooks:

> Humor must not professedly teach, and it must not professedly preach, but it must do both if it would live forever. . . . I have always preached. . . . If the humor came of its own accord and uninvited, I have allowed it a place in my sermon, but I was not writing the sermon for the sake of the humor. I should have written the sermon just the same, whether any humor applied for admission or not.[4]

One need only read Henry Steele Commager's description of the American character in *The American Mind: An Interpretation of American Thought and Character Since the 1880's* to presume the effectiveness of Twain's rhetoric.[5] Commager's description of the American character at the end of the nineteenth century mirrored the message Twain began preaching more than twenty years earlier. Commager saw the American as "democratic and egalitarian"; one who believed that the "self-made man, not the heir, was the hero."[6] According to the historian, the nineteenth-century American disrespected authority, ridiculed culture, and only conformed when it came to morals. Commager's characterization of American humor accurately describes the humor in Twain's works: It tended toward exaggeration, the outrageous, and celebrated the ludicrous and the grotesque. "It was democratic and leveling, [taking the] side of the underdog and [ridiculing] the great and the proud."[7] Commager comments that humor was "not only a positive but a notorious national trait; as pervasive as optimism and carelessness—and closely allied with both."[8]

The connection between Twain's message and Commager's description of the American character serves to illustrate Twain's effective use of the rhetoric of identification. Through his oral presentations, this native son, whose own character was honed by homespun American experiences from his pioneering parents and frontier life, spread his view of the world. Undoubtedly, he contributed a great deal toward the development of American nationalism. His message and his ethos were one; Mark Twain was the Representative American.

Twain's speeches were successful chiefly because of his comprehension of the communication process. He learned the art of oratory first hand, not at a school for elocutionary training as most of his counterparts did. Through careful observation and practice, Mark Twain concluded notions about public speaking that presaged modern rhetorical theory.[9] He once commented, "I know a great many secrets about audiences—secrets not to be gotten out of books, but acquired only by experience."[10] In contrast to the systems taught at the popular schools of oratory, which emphasized the importance of the speaker, the focus of Twain's performance was on the audience, specifically the interaction between speaker and listeners.

Twain loved the social interaction of the speech event. Although he complained about the hard life of the lecturer, especially the travel, one-night stands, and loneliness, he was fascinated by the phenomenon. In 1867 he wrote of his enthusiasm for public speaking in letters to the *Alta California*, in 1867. He spoke of his excursions to Brooklyn to study the styles of preachers Henry Ward Beecher and the Reverend Dr. Chapin, expressing that he was particularly impressed with Dr. Chapin's power. Twain reasoned that in every listener's head seemed to be an invisible wire connected to a battery in the preacher's head, for his audience looked spellbound.[11] Twain sought to develop this sense of audience, and he did so most successfully. As his friend and renowned critic William Dean Howells wrote, "He knew all the stops in that simple instrument man, and there is no doubt that these results were accurately intended from his unerring knowledge."[12]

Twain learned that for a speaker to achieve his purpose, he must adjust his discourse to relate directly to the listeners—their needs, their experiences, and their ability to relate to the speaker. In other words, Twain's speech events involved achieving consubstantiality, the term Kenneth Burke uses to describe the rhetoric of identification. Burke contends, "You persuade a man only insofar as you can talk his language by speech, gesture, tonality, order, image, attitude, idea, identifying your way with his."[13] Twain's art, according to Paine, "was of the sort that made the hearer forget that he was not being personally entertained by a new and wonderful friend, who had come there for his particular benefit."[14]

Twain's speeches were rhetorical acts because they addressed rhetorical situations.[15] In his earlier presentations, in particular, Twain was concerned with the social and cultural life in nineteenth-century America, especially the development of the popular culture and the establishment of a unified American culture. Later he brought his libertarian views to political issues. Overall, Twain's fundamental regard was for humankind. He spoke to promote and defend basic human rights. Twain's target audience was stated clearly by him: "I have never tried in even one single instance, to help cultivate the cultivated classes. I was not equipped for it, either by native gifts or training. And I never had any ambition in that direction, but always hunted for bigger game—the masses."[16]

Underlying all his works is his deep compassion for what he later angrily termed "the damned human race." Twain was critical of the practice of civilizing. Civilization corrupts, distorts reality, and encourages hypocrisy. He believed that man in his natural state was more moral. In the "Sandwich Island Lecture," for example, he reveals the moral superiority of the natives in light of attempts made to civilize them. In two toasts, "On Adam" and "The Babies," he proclaims the superiority of those untouched by civilization. Twain acknowledges his preference for the first human, Adam: "[T]he only solitary celebrity in our family. I stand up for him on account of his sterling private virtues, as a man and a citizen."[17] "The Babies," addressed to powerful members of the army, including General Grant, salutes our common beginnings.[18] The exigencies Twain addressed involved moral questions, from the superior attitude of the American Victorians to the policy of imperialism. Incidents depicting man's inhumanity to man motivated him to mount the platform. Twain regarded himself as a reformer. Twain's motives were clearly rhetorical.

At the conclusion of "The Savage Club Dinner Speech," delivered in London, on July 6, 1907, Twain eloquently summarized his sentiments about the superiority of the common man. Referring to the love for him expressed by the English, he noted the hearty welcome from the stevedores as his ship docked, those who "do the heavy labor in the world, and save you and me from having to do it":

> They are the men, who, with their hands, build empires and make them prosper. It is because of them that the others are wealthy and can live in luxury. They received me with a "Hurrah!" that went to my heart. They are the men that build civilization, and without them no civilization can be built. So I came first to the authors and creators of civilization, and I blessedly end in this happy meeting with the Savages who destroy it.[19]

Twain's method for communicating his motives reflect Burke's thesis:

> A speaker persuades an audience by the use of stylistic identifications; his act of persuasion may be for the purpose of causing the audience to identify itself with the speaker's interests; and the speaker draws an identification of interest to establish rapport between himself and his audience.[20]

His style, in substance and delivery, was carefully developed to effect change through identification. If the audience could not identify with his subject, then it certainly could identify with his manner.

Twain's most effective rhetorical device was humor. On the surface, he used humor to develop a rapport with his listeners. Through laughter, their feedback, he could measure his effectiveness. Twain also used humor as a means of empathy. He encouraged his listeners to laugh—at him, at authority, and, most importantly, at themselves. His humor tended to be self-deprecating, in the mode of the frontier. However, humor played a more vital role in Twain's strategy. With such stylistic tools as irony, hyperbole, anecdote, comic pose, and dialect, Twain built his satirical works. These devices encouraged his audience to question conventional behavior through absurdity and incongruity. Thus, the self-righteous were exposed as inferior, causing Twain's target audience to feel superior. In other words, Twain's humor functioned for moral reconstitution.

Twain explains his reason for using such humorous devices:

> I have found that when I speak the truth, I am not believed, and that I have never told a lie so big that someone had sublime confidence in my veracity. I have, therefore, been forced by fate to adopt fiction as a medium of truth. Most liars lie for the love of the lie; I lie for the love of truth. I disseminate my true views by means of a series of apparently humorous and mendacious stories.[21]

The term that commonly has been used to describe Twain's humor is "irreverent." According to Henry Nash Smith, "Most people who prided themselves on having a cultivated taste considered vernacular humor to be vulgar, if indeed not actually immoral."[22] Louis Budd attests that "[I]rreverence is always needed to challenge the status quo which entrenches itself in sacred tradition and to strip away the cliches that cover up evil or just insensitivity."[23] True to the American character, Twain viewed himself as a social leveler, one who needed to debunk all social pretense for the promotion of democracy. With these humorous devices, Twain exposed the hypocrisy behind the sanctimonious dictates of conventional society. For example, Twain lampooned romantic notions about the Old World, as in the "The American Vandal Abroad," lecture[24] and vacuous moral teachings, as in the "Advice to Youth" speech.[25]

Specifically, the chief target of Twain's satire is the establishment, those institutions and organizations that sit in judgement over the masses, namely the church, the government, literary critics, and so on. For example, he ridicules the church in the "Sandwich Islands Lecture" and his "The American Vandal Abroad" lecture; the government in his "Edmund Burke and Croker" speech; and the literati in the Whittier's Birthday speech and "On Foreign Critics."[26]

Twain used anecdote for identification. With folksy stories, many of which he picked up from his Western experiences, Twain engaged his audience in a hilarious romp as he slowly and craftily fed the purposely disjointed plotline to them. Deftly, he interwove pathos with humor. Excellent examples can be found in the "Roughing It Lecture,"[27] such as "His Grandfather's Old Ram," "The Mexican Plug," and, his most popular, "The Celebrated Jumping Frog." Some of these stories are told with Twain adopting the comic pose of the Tenderfoot, the innocent, yet ignorant newcomer who is made the butt of the conniving know-it-all. The listeners laugh at this characterization of themselves, the "real" Americans, who, despite their lot in life, prove to be the better human beings. In sum, Twain's use of the comic pose achieves his egalitarian motive for humbling the "superior" and exalting the "inferior."

Another stylistic form used by Twain to humble the so-called mighty is hyperbole. His grossly exaggerated description of the demise of Simon Wheeler in the "Roughing It Lecture" is an excellent example. This technique was purely American. As Walter Blair explains in his study of American humor, "[F]or almost two centuries the best way to make an idea tasty to most of the people of this country has been to serve it up with a sauce of native-grown humor and horse sense."[28]

Paramount to Twain's rhetorical strategy was his delivery. "Manner is everything,"[29] Twain once remarked, and he exemplified this contention to the end. Above all, Twain was a consummate public performer. "On the platform," noted Howells, "he was the great and finished actor which he probably would not have been on the stage."[30] His innate ability to enchant an audience was perceived at his very first public lecture. The review in the *New York Herald*, May 7, 1867, remarked that Twain's delivery was "so pleasing . . . that he, in a moment's acquaintance with his audience, makes them his friends . . ."[31]

Notable contemporaries such as Archibald Henderson wrote that Twain possessed "the gift of innate eloquence." He was "the master of the art of moving, touching, swaying an audience. Twain's insight into the mysterious springs of humor, of passion, and of pathos almost seem like divination."[32] An article in 1896 concluded a description of Twain's performance talent: "To have read Mark Twain is a delight. But to have seen and heard him is a joy not readily to be forgotten."[33]

His platform style, which was in stark contrast to his elocution-trained counterparts, was definitely the major component of his rhetorical strategy. His "apparently artless art"[34] had great popular appeal. By obviously violating the conventions of delivery by dispensing with all prescribed formalities—a proper introduction, the appropriate posture, and diction—Twain maintained his rebellion against the dominant culture. At the same time, this behavior reinforced his identification with the audience. Twain's posturing was apparent to his audience, and that heightened the humor of his presentations. Lampooning the Victorians' veneration of sincerity reinforced the moral qualities he consistently preached.

His performances were crafted with meticulous care. He planned his style to achieve what he called "the captivating naturalness of an impromptu narration."[35] One device he relied on was the use of the surprise. He knew that keeping the listeners in suspense heightens the mood of the event and encourages greater audience involvement. The audience reveled in not knowing what to expect, especially when his lectures were advertised as "The trouble begins tonight." So, particularly in the early years, when he was promoting his reputation as a humorist, he would prepare his audience for his message by using what today's comedians call "shtick." That is, when it came time for Twain to make his entrance, he would stumble onto the stage and stare embarrassingly at the audience. He ended his presentations in similar fashion, for example, by stumbling toward the wrong exit.

To further heighten the effect of his humor, Twain relied on another element of surprise—the pause. Twain believed that the pause was the most effective speaking device. He described it as that "impressive silence, that eloquent silence, that geometrically progressive silence which often achieves a desired effect where no combination of words howsoever felicitous could accomplish it."[36] He was most concerned about the timing of the pause, and he carefully watched the facial expressions of the listeners to determine the right moment to bring it to an end. Twain explained, "If the pause is too short the impressive point is passed, and the audience has had time to divine that a surprise is intended—and you can't surprise them, of course."[37] According to one observer, "Twain knew how to make one second of silence outweigh a hundred words."[38]

Another part of Twain's strategy was the selection of his verbal codes. Choosing the right word from the almost right word is the "difference between the lightning bug and the lightning."[39] As Edwin Black explains in his article "The Second Persona": "The association between an idiom and an ideology is much more than a matter of arbitrary convention or inexplicable accident. It suggests that there are strong and multifarious links between a style and an outlook."[40]

Twain's mode of delivery was extemporaneous, rather than the manuscript style. Howells reports that in the early years he tried to memorize passages with a unique system of mnemonics:

> On the dinner-table a certain succession of knife, spoon, salt-cellar, and butter-plate symbolized a train of ideas, and the billiard-table a ball, a cue, and a piece of chalk serve the same purpose. With a diagram of these printed on the brain he had full command of the phrases which his excogitation had attached to them, and which embodied the ideas in perfect form.[41]

Twain purposely refused to use a manuscript because he believed it detracted from the effect of spontaneity, which he found most effective in relating to the audience:

> Print is the proper vehicle for written speech, but the moment "talk" is put into print you recognize that it is not what it was when you read it; you perceive that an immense something has disappeared

from it. That's its soul. [W]ritten things . . . have to be limbered up, broken up, colloquialized, and turned into common forms of unpremeditated talk—otherwise they will bore the house, not entertain it.[42]

A thorough description of Twain and his performance style can be found in an article that appeared in the April 25, 1886, issue of *The Critic*:

> [F]or the most part, he talks in low, slow, conversational tones, at times he rises to real bursts of eloquence—not the polished grandiloquent eloquence of the average American speaker, but the eloquence conveyed in simple words and phrases, and promoted by some deep and sincerely felt sentiment. Mark Twain steals unobtrusively on to the platform, dressed in the regulation evening-clothes, with the trouser-pockets cut high up, into which he occasionally drives both hands. He bows with a quiet dignity to the roaring cheers which greet him at every "At Home." Then, with natural, unaffected gesture, and with scarcely any prelude, he gets under way with his first story. He is a picturesque figure on the stage. His long, shaggy, white hair surmounts a face full of intellectual fire. The eyes, arched with bushy brows, and which seem to be closed most of the time while he is speaking, flash out now and then from their deep sockets with a genial, kindly, pathetic look, and the face is deeply drawn with the furrows accumulated during an existence of sixty years. He talks in short sentences, with a peculiar smack of the lips at the end of each. His language is just that of his books, full of the quaintest Americanisms . . . . His figure is rather slight, not above middle height, and the whole man suggests an utter lack of physical energy. . . . Mark Twain stands perfectly still in one place during the whole of the time he is talking to the audience. He rarely moves his arms, unless it is to adjust his spectacles or to show by action how a certain thing was done. His characteristic attitude is to stand quite still, with the right arm across the abdomen and the left resting on it and supporting his chin. In this way he talks on for nearly two hours; and, while the audience is laughing uproariously, he never by any chance relapses into a smile.[43]

The more experienced he became, according to his official biographer, Albert Bigelow Paine, the less it seemed so, "for it was his naturalness, his apparent lack of art, that was his greatest charm."[44] However, a letter to his wife in 1870, during his second lecture series, indicates Twain's awareness of the power of his image. He told of an experience when he walked on stage and said nothing, just stood there, and the audience responded with thunderous applause. "An audience captured in that way *belongs* to the speaker, body and soul, for the rest of the evening. Therefore, isn't it worth the taking of some perilous chances on?"[45]

People from all around desired to experience his captivating style. Twain's ethos became his most persuasive appeal. His message and his persona blended, becoming one. According to Louis Budd, "the blinding magic of his personality,"[46] projected him from mere mortal to national symbol. He was proclaimed the "quintessence; the throbbing avatar of national virtues."[47] Gamaliel Bradford saw him as "the bard . . . who gathered up in himself, almost unconsciously, the life and spirit of a whole nation and poured it forth, more as a voice, an instrument, than a deliberate artist."[48]

Twain's platform performances are indeed rhetorical acts. His prescient awareness of the communication process moved him to be most concern with audience response. His common approach, in posture, language, and substance, persuaded the masses to identify with him, to see themselves, the "true" Americans, in this representative figure. Twain's motives for speaking focused on effecting social change, and he was convincing. All elements of his presentations—from the folksy anecdote to the slipshod stance and slowed diction—promoted his rhetorical strategy. Above all, his aim was that of rhetoric, as defined by Richard Weaver in *The Ethics of Rhetoric*: "Rhetoric at its truest seeks to perfect men by showing them better versions of themselves."[49]

Mark Twain, 1890. Courtesy of The Mark Twain Project, The Bancroft Library.

3
Critical Analysis: Lectures

> "In truth, a man cannot be a popular lecturer who does not plant himself upon the eternal principles of justice. He must be a democrat, a believer in and an advocate of the equal rights of men."
>
> —*Atlantic Monthly*, 1865

For over forty years Mark Twain pursued his "alternate career," as he termed his experience as a platform performer. From his first public lecture in 1866 to his final speech in 1909, Twain presented what may be classified as lectures and occasional speeches, particularly after-dinner speeches, to a variety of audiences located in diverse settings—from small, shoddy frontier towns to the courts of European and Asian nobility, from the closed recesses of exclusive men's clubs to the controlled camps of convicts. Despite the variations in style, structure, and tone of his talks, Mark Twain's democratic appeal remained constant. His message extolling the virtues of autonomy and authenticity can be found in every discourse.

Mark Twain began his platform career during the period of the popular lecture. Begun in the 1820s, just about every town, especially in the East, had a lyceum association that booked speakers for "courses." Six or eight speakers made up each "course," and the presentations ranged from orations and sermons to recitations and travel narratives. These circuits of public speech served the purpose of educating the expanding population. Come the lecture season, from October to March, an array of pundits, prophets, reformers, preachers, and professors took to the road. Among the more successful speakers were Ralph Waldo Emerson, William James, Petroleum V. Nasby, Artemus Ward, Anna Dickinson, and, of course, Mark Twain.

Uniquely American, the popular lecture was considered the "most purely democratic of all our democratic institutions."[1] The popular speaker was one with a keen sense of audience, one who endeavored to relate to all of the auditors, the educated and the uneducated, creating a common bond by focusing on common, uniquely American experiences. Above all, the lecture system is credited with the spread of the American idiom and American culture, resulting in the development of the strong spirit of nationalism that fortified the United States by the close of the nineteenth century.

Much of the credit for the development of American nationalism belongs to Mark Twain. His humorous lectures spread basic democratic principles to the delight of his listeners. Through his rhetoric of identification, he became the embodiment of the American spirit—the Representative American.

Mark Twain's lectures, on the whole, were prepared more fastidiously than his later performances. Three of them, the most successful, are concerned with travel adventures. With the "innocent eye" of the common man, Twain relates how he sees the world. All include mixtures of humor and pathos with touches of eloquence exemplified in breathtaking description. For example, in the midst of his humorous discussions on life-as-he-saw-it on the Sandwich Islands, Twain inserts a description of a volcanic eruption that readily demonstrates his writing talent. Twain also discloses his literary talent with his description of Athens by moonlight in "The American Vandal Abroad" lecture and with his description of Lake Tahoe, Nevada, in the "Roughing It Lecture."[2] These lectures also followed a similar organizational pattern—an introduction that presented the topic, a cogent development of the topic, and a conclusion focused on a beautiful description, a moral, or an admonition.

"SANDWICH ISLANDS LECTURE"

Twain's first public lecture launched his reputation as a popular public speaker. At the age of thirty, he presented the "Sandwich Islands Lecture" on October 2, 1866, in San Francisco. This popular talk was delivered intermittently thereafter until December 8, 1873, almost 100 times in the United States and England, where he announced the title as "Our Fellow Savages of the Sandwich Islands." The material for this lecture evolved from Twain's four-month visit to Hawaii in 1866 and his twenty-five letters from there published in the Sacramento *Union*. Twain planned to write a book on his travels when he returned to San Francisco, but he had no job and first needed to make some money. At one dollar a head, a packed house at Maguire's Academy of Music proved the solution. The audience, those members who came because they enjoyed Twain's newspaper reports, as well as those who came out of curiosity created particularly by Twain's advertisement "The trouble begins at eight," were not disappointed at all. One newspaper, the *Golden Era*, declared his superiority to the contemporary favorite Artemus Ward: "From here on, Artemus can hide his diminished luminary under several bushels; he is as a penn'orth of tallow to a mammoth circus chandelier."[3] From then on, Twain classified his platform performances as his "alternate career."[4]

Needing money for the *Quaker City* Mediterranean cruise he was hired to report on for the *Alta California*, and realizing the impact the publicity for the speaking event could have on his reputation as a writer, Twain prepared the "Sandwich Island Lecture" for his Eastern debut. Thousands filled the lecture halls in New York and Brooklyn, particularly curious about the author of "The Celebrated Jumping Frog." They were not disappointed. According to a review in the *New York Times*, on May 6, 1867, "[S]eldom has so large an audience been so uniformly pleased as the one that listened to Mark Twain's quaint remarks last evening."[5] The *New York Herald* commented that his manner and style of delivery "is so pleasing and acceptable that he, in a moment's acquaintance with his audience, makes them his friends, and with constant laughter and genuine enthusiasm carries them along with him to the end, dismissing them in the happiest possible frame of mind."[6] One reviewer commented that Twain's perspective was that of an "ordinary man of the world" who exhibited folksy American humor. He found Twain's skill of anecdote and command of the American idiom and his powers of mimicry most entertaining.[7]

Underlying the humor in the "Sandwich Islands Lecture" are indications of Twain's perception of society, in particular, those aspects on which he shapes all of his rhetoric. Twain's method is satire. In the persona of the common man, Twain uses irony, hyperbole, sarcasm, and shocking detail to deliver his message. His message questions the morality of imperialism, specifically that of the dominant culture's attempts to civilize the natives.

Right after he jokingly introduces himself, to set the tone of his discourse, Twain states his purpose concisely: "The Sandwich Islands will be the subject of my lecture—when I get to it—and I shall endeavor to tell the truth . . ." Twain then shocks the audience to attention by chatting matter-of-factly about what the listeners would consider grotesque. For example, he mentions his opinion on seeing a piece of ancient sculpture of a "freshly skinned man": "It looked so natural; it looked as if it was in pain, and you know a freshly skinned man would naturally look that way."

Continuing his apparent diversion from the topic, Twain intensifies the humorous mood with another of his devices: mixing pathos with humor. In the manner of the frontier, Twain tells an anecdote about his reaction about discovering that he was in the same room with a dead man. After he "yarns" the scary situation, he paints a humorous image: "I went away from there.

I didn't hurry—simply went out of the window—and took the sash along with me. I didn't need the sash, but it was handier to take it than to leave it."

Throughout this factual discourse about the geography, economy, and culture of the islands, Twain weaves his satire. For example, he expresses his suspicion of the white man's intrusion into native cultures by describing the occupation with an ironic twist:

> When these islands were discovered the population was about 400,000, but the white man came and brought various complicated diseases, and education, and civilization, and all sorts of calamities, and consequently the population began to drop off with commendable activity. Forty years ago they were reduced to 200,000, and the educational and civilizing facilities being increased they dwindled down to 55,000, and it is proposed to send a few more missionaries and finish them.

Then Twain concludes sarcastically, "When they pick up and leave we will take possession as lawful heirs."

Twain compares the natives with the self-righteous Victorians in order to demonstrate the moral superiority of these primitive people. For example, in reaction to the obsession with clothing the naked Kanakas for the sake of propriety, Twain innocently observes: "[B]ut they are not vicious at all, they are good people." He hurls a hit at the false behavior of Victorian women with his description of the native women: "When women meet each other in the road, they run and kiss and hug each other, and they don't blackguard each other behind each other's backs." He illustrates that although the natives' customs differ, they are decent human beings:

> They will feed you on baked dog, or poi, or raw fish, or raw salt pork, fricasseed cats—all the luxuries of the season . . . Perhaps, now, this isn't a captivating feast at first glance, but it is offered in all sincerity, and with the best motives in the world.

Attacking the bigotry of the dominant culture, Twain remarks about the natives' peculiar custom for "calling any woman mother they take a liking to—no matter what her color or politics."

Twain uses hyperbole to criticize the so-called "good" claimed to have been done by the missionaries:

> The American missionaries "set the common man free . . . taught the whole nation to read and write with facility, in the native tongue. I don't suppose there is today a single uneducated person above eight years of age in the Sandwich Islands. It is the best educated

> country in the world, I believe, not excepting portions of the United States.

After that pronouncement, Twain proceeds to describe the habits of the natives such as their eating "baked dog" and "fricasseed cat." On their cannibalism, he remarks, for shock effect, "They didn't eat Captain Cook—or if they did, it was only for fun."

Twain's distrust of government is clearly evident in this early speech. He reacts negatively to imperialistic plans, sarcastically complaining that the natives will make the wrong kind of voters:

> They will do everything wrong end first. . . . Instead of fostering and encouraging a judicious system of railway speculation, and all that sort of thing, they will elect the most incorruptible men to Congress. Yes, they will turn everything upside down.

Undoubtedly, the "Sandwich Islands Lecture" is more than an entertaining presentation. It is a well-crafted rhetorical act. Mark Twain's beliefs in the natural virtues of authenticity and autonomy were ingrained in his self-system. They are fundamental to understanding all his creative works.

The "Sandwich Island Lecture" is also an excellent example of oratory because of its literary qualities. Twain's description of the natural attributes of the land is a paean to the moral supremacy of nature over humankind. The descriptions of the volcano Kilauea's omnipotent power and of the sensual splendor of these tropical isles demonstrate Twain's inventive talent.

The success of the first performance of this lecture boosted Twain's popularity as well as his finances. He dubbed it the turning point of his life. His reputation as an American original was established, and people clamored to hear more of him. They were fascinated with his talent and his refreshing point of view. He also gained a greater appreciation of the speaking purpose and process that developed his oral style of expression.

"THE AMERICAN VANDAL ABROAD" LECTURE

Twain's second lecture, "The American Vandal Abroad," follows the pattern set by the first. It was derived from his experiences as a passenger on the steamer *Quaker City*'s excursion to the Mediterranean, from June 8 to November 19, 1867. Assigned to report on the trip for the *Alta California*, Twain's letters were published every Sunday in the *Alta* and were copied freely by other California papers. These letters served as the foundation for his forthcoming book *Innocents Abroad*, from which Twain claimed to have "smouched" the lecture.

"The American Vandal Abroad" was performed during the lyceum season of November 17, 1868, to March 3, 1869. Twain, with comic satire, addresses the penchant of some Americans to pay sentimental homage to the Old World. He describes the Vandal's grand tour as superficial, one of rushing through countries and collecting souvenirs indiscriminately. By revealing their ignorance and questioning their motives, Twain is ridiculing the Victorians' notions of cultural superiority. He attempts to unify the American culture by debunking long-revered icons of Europe. With a vernacular perspective, Twain functions as social leveler. He moves his audience toward self-awareness by causing them to laugh at themselves through the Vandal. As usual, the purpose of his presentation is to teach and to preach.

Twain describes these Vandals as "the roving, independent, free-and-easy character of that class of traveling Americans who are *not* elaborately educated, cultivated, and refined, and gilded and filigreed with the ineffable graces of the first society." He explains his choice of topic sarcastically: "The best class of our countrymen who go abroad keep us well posted about their doings in foreign lands, but their brethren Vandals cannot sing their own praises or publish their adventures."

In a letter to one of his major supporters, Mrs. Fairbanks, Twain explains his characterization of the Vandal: "I treat him gently & goodnaturedly, except that I give him *one* savage blast for aping foreign ways."[8] Twain describes him to his audience with dramatic simplicity:

> He tries everything . . . is very gullible. . . . He is proud and looks proud. . . . He does not fail to let the public know that he is an American. This is not a fault. It is commendable. I have seen him in the company of kings and queens, lords and popes. He is always self-possessed, always untouched, unabashed—even in the presence of the Sphinx.

Speaking through the Vandal, Twain criticizes the sentimental veneration of religious icons such as holy relics and the painting of *The Last Supper* by recording the Vandal's matter-of-fact reaction: "If a cathedral does not have a splinter of the Cross or a piece of a saint it "has no charm for *him*." *The Last Supper* is "a perfect old nightmare of a picture and he wouldn't give forty dollars for a million like it."

Twain has a delightful time disclosing the fraud behind many so-called sacred artifacts:

> They have many holy relics in the Cathedral of Milan. The priest showed us two of St. Paul's fingers and one of St. Peter's; and a

> bone of Judas Iscariot—it was a black one—and bones and little vessels of blood of St. John, St. Mark and several other of the disciples. They keep these relics in vials, in a glass case, and have them labeled as we often see geological specimens. And they showed us a handkerchief in which the Savior had left the impression of his face (we saw another in Rome afterward), and a piece of the stone the angels rolled away from the door of the Holy Sepulchre (we saw the whole of the stone afterward in Jerusalem)—and a part of the real crown of thorns (we saw a whole one at Notre Dame in Paris)—and a fragment of the purple robe worn by the Savior, a nail from the True Cross and a picture of the Virgin and Child painted by the veritable hand of St. Luke.

Throughout the narrative, Twain lampoons the ignorance of the tourist. For example, he describes the Vandal's desire to visit Venice in order to see such sights as the Bridge of Sighs and "the Rialto, where Shylock used to loan money on human flesh and other collateral."

Intermingled in this burlesque are eloquent passages of description, verifications of Twain's literary talent. He paints beautiful word pictures of Athens and Venice at night. For example, he recalls Athens: "[T]he silent city was flooded with the mellowest light that ever streamed from the moon, and seemed like some living creature wrapped in peaceful slumber." He remembers Venice after everyone has gone home:

> [W]e have lonely stretches of glittering water, of stately buildings, of blotting shadows, of weird stone faces creeping into the moonlight, of deserted bridges, of motionless boats at anchor—and over all broods that mysterious stillness, that stealthy quiet, that befits so well this old dreaming Venice!

Twain's final recollection of his travels is his perception of Alexander II, Autocrat of Russia. Like a true democrat, he shatters the image of autocracy by describing the Emperor as being "like an ordinary mortal." Speaking with American pride, Twain explains:

> This man's slightest word is law to 70,000,000 of human beings! . . . Yet where I stood, worm of the dust as I am, I could have overturned this god—I could have knocked this colossus down with my feeble fist—but I restrained myself.

Following the form of lyceum lectures, "The American Vandal Abroad" concludes with a moral; however, Twain uses verbal irony to reinforce his democratic message:

> If there is a moral to this lecture it is an injunction to all Vandals to *travel.* I am glad the American Vandal *goes* abroad. It does him good. It makes a better *man* of him. It rubs out a multitude of his old unworthy biases and prejudices. . . . [I]t broadens his views of men and things. . . . Contact with men of various nations and many creeds, teaches him that there are *other* people in the world besides his own little clique, and other opinions as worthy of attention and respect as his own. He finds that he and *his* are not the most momentous matters in the universe. . . . [H]e begins to learn the best lesson of all—that one which culminates in the conviction that God puts *something* good and something lovable in every man His hands create—that the world is not a cold, harsh, cruel prison-house, stocked with all manner of selfishness and hate and wickedness.

Twain justified the irreverent nature of his humor. He adamantly believed, like the average American, that a discriminating irreverence was the creator and protector of human liberty.

The lecture proved more significant than Twain estimated. First, it further increased his popularity. His reputation grew from that of Western journalist to national humorist, from "Wild Humorist of the Pacific Slope" to the "Moralist of the Main." He was asked to join James Redpath's Boston Lyceum Bureau, enabling him to make a great deal of money and spread his reputation. He was now convinced that he could please Eastern audiences as well as those in the West. His book, *Innocents Abroad*, was published four months after the tour closed, contributing to his worldwide reputation.

"ROUGHING IT LECTURE"

Twain's most popular lecture was the "Roughing It Lecture," which he performed midway into the lecture season of 1871-1872 and later in England in 1873. The lecture season of 1871-1872, which Twain described in a letter to Mrs. Fairbanks as "the most detestable campaign that ever was,"[9] did not begin well. Twain's new lecture, titled "Reminiscences of Some Uncommonplace Characters I Have Chanced to Meet," did not have the appeal of the first two. After three disappointing performances in eastern Pennsylvania, he abandoned it. In Washington, D.C., he resumed lecturing on only one on the uncommonplace characters, Artemus Ward. Again the lecture was unsuccessful; critics called it improper because Twain was speaking about a dead man in a burlesque style. Finally, Twain decided to use parts from his forthcoming book, *Roughing It*. It worked. Twain wrote, "Tried it last night. Suits me tip top."[10]

The "Roughing It Lecture" is a narrative about Twain's experiences in the far West. He presents a detailed description of life in this wild territory, recounting the rigors of human survival as well as the opportunities to get rich quick. Interspersed throughout this travelogue are engaging description of the dynamic beauty of the scenery.

The popularity of this lecture stemmed from the curiosity the world had about this land. All kinds of stories flowed from the region about the challenges of the rugged terrain and harsh climate, the dangers of Indian attacks, the lawlessness of desperados, and the lure of the silver mines. These reports tended to romanticize the life where "men were men" and only the fit survived. Eastern and English audiences craved to hear tales of this fantasy land.

In addition to the appeal of the subject, this lecture attracted large audiences because of the storyteller. Similar to the "Sandwich Islands Lecture" and "The American Vandal Abroad," Twain recounts his experience with a vernacular perspective. He is the neophyte who seeks adventure without prior study and preparation. Assuming the comic pose of the Tenderfoot, Twain recounts how he stumbled through his days with the amazement of the ignorant. This characterization encourages the listeners to identify with him; they experience the Wild West vicariously.

With this lecture Twain popularized the image of the American, the character that had become an international curiosity. In response to Crèvecoeur's famous question "What then is the American, this new man?" the "Roughing It Lecture," and, of course, the book *Roughing It*, demonstrated that the American is adventurous, courageous, enterprising, and close to nature. The lecture also showed that he is a survivor who delights in laughing at his own foibles. The "new man" is practical and fiercely independent; he focuses on the challenges of reality with commonsense logic. Above all, the American loves his freedom.

To set the humorous mood and also to define the moral superiority of the chief character in his narrative, the common man, Twain begins the discourse by ridiculing conventional introductions. He introduces himself in the effusive style of these introductions as "a gentleman whose great learning, whose historical accuracy, whose devotion to science, and whose veneration for the truth, are only equaled by his high moral character and his majestic presence." Then, to expose the superficiality of such introductions, Twain contrasts it with the blunt honesty and the commonsense logic of "the one public introduction that seemed to me just exactly the thing—an introduction brimful of grace. Why, it was a sort of inspiration. . . . sensible to the backbone":

Ladies and gentlemen, I shan't fool away any unnecessary time in

> this introduction. I don't know anything about this man; at least I know only two things; one is, that he has never been in the penitentiary; and the other is, I don't know why.

Twain stimulates American pride with his eloquent descriptions of the natural beauty of the land. For example, he describes the majesty of the Rocky Mountains and its "celebrated South Pass." He must have held his audience spellbound as he describes the first time he saw a storm occur in that region:

> I could watch that storm break forth down there; could see the lightnings flash, the sheeted rain drifting along the canon's side, and hear the thunder crash upon crash, reverberating among a thousand rocky cliffs.

Twain heightens the allure of the West with a compelling word-picture of Lake Tahoe, which he describes as "the noblest, loveliest inland lake in the world":

> I have seen some of the world's celebrated lakes and they bear no comparison with Tahoe. There it is, a sheet of perfectly pure, limpid water, lifted up 6,300 feet above the sea—a vast oval mirror framed in a wall of snow-clad mountain peaks, above the common world.

Like an impassioned evangelist, the master raconteur reaches into the very souls of his listeners with his mesmerizing view of the total experience:

> Could you but see the morning breaking there, gilding those snowy summits and then creeping gradually along the slopes until it sets the lake and woodlands free from mist, all agleam, you would see old Nature, the master artist, painting those dissolving views on the still water and finally grouping all these features into a complete picture. Every little dell, the mountains with their dome-turned pinnacles, the cataracts and drifting clouds, are all exquisitely photographed on the burnished surface of the lake, suffused with the softest and richest color.

As usual, Twain checks any risk of losing the humorous mood of his masterful work by injecting shots of folksy humor. For example, the magnificent description of Lake Tahoe is followed by the Tenderfoot's sales pitch about the air as "a cure of for consumptives": "If it don't cure them, I will bury them—I shall be glad to do it. I will give them a funeral that will be a comfort to them as long as they live. But it *will* cure them." To fortify his belief, the Tenderfoot tells the tale of a miraculous cure with characteristic exaggeration.

Twain appeals to the enterprising nature of the American by describing the mineral wealth in Nevada, quoting the price of some silver-ladened quartz at $2,000 per ton. He tells of his striking it rich and then losing it just as quickly through circumstances: "It don't seem possible that there could be three as big fools in one small town, but we were there, and I was one of them."

The most concentrated source of Twain's humor in the lecture is found in his recollection of the story of the Mexican plug. This story typifies American humor through characterization, style of expression, and use of exaggeration. Twain intensifies his humor with his usual combination of pathos and humor. Posing as the Tenderfoot, Twain warns his listeners of being duped by the local con men by painting a hilarious picture of his sad experience. The audience was moved to laugh at his and their gullibility and hard times.

This story describes the trusting nature of the Tenderfoot, who innocently believes that the broken down horse he paid too much for is "a genuine Mexican plug" who could "outbuck any horse in America. . . . any horse in the world." As soon as this novice equestrian mounts the horse, the horse bucks, throwing him "one hundred and eighty yards" into the air. After two more violent bucks, the horse ran off, leaving the Tenderfoot high in the air. He heard a man close to him remark, "Oh, don't he buck!" Twain ends with the Tenderfoot's forlorn utterance: "So that was 'bucking.'"

Twain varied his presentations of this lecture with similar tall tales. Stories such as "The Celebrated Jumping Frog" and "His Grandfather's Old Ram" were in popular demand.

Twain's most popular story is the one about the jumping frog. This story, first printed in a Western newspaper, the Virginia City *Enterprise*, was republished in the East, igniting interest in Twain's humor. Like "The Mexican Plug," this tale lampoons the ignorance of the inhabitants of a mining town. Its plot also involves the deceitful practice of swindling, but this time the local swindler is swindled by a stranger. Jim Smiley's "jumpingest" frog Daniel Webster was outjumped. Smiley becomes a victim of his own con game, done in by his own gullibility. The lesson from these highly entertaining stories combines self-realization with the need for education.

In "His Grandfather's Old Ram," Twain lightly buffoons life in small-town America by describing the innocent ignorance of its inhabitants. One of the anecdotes he relates deals with a kindly woman who would lend her glass eye to an old lady who had none "to receive company in":

> [I]t warn't big enough . . . [I]t would get twisted around in the socket, and look up, maybe, or out to one side, and every which way, while t'other one was looking as straight ahead as a spy glass.

Mark Twain prepared two other lecture tours that proved disappointing. One, "Artemus Ward," was a tribute to the humorist Artemus Ward, on whom, by the way, Twain tended to pattern his early performances. Delivered several times in the East and the middle West during the lecture season of 1871-1872, his lecture was eventually replaced with material Twain had collected for his new book, *Roughing It*. The other, "Morals Lecture," was not a new creation but a collection of old stories loosely joined together with playful comments on moral principles. Twain used this lecture for his round-the-world speaking tour, which began in Cleveland, July 15, 1895. As usual, his reason for embarking on this tour was to pay debts, this time those incurred from his failed business ventures. According to Fred Lorch, no manuscript text of this talk has been found, "if, indeed, there ever was one."[11]

Overall, the three lectures discussed here can be credited for Mark Twain's soaring popularity. They helped sell his books and his philosophy. Especially, they served to encourage a worldwide fascination for this new person, the American. In addition, Twain's platform experience honed his sense of audience and his oral style of writing, which resulted in his great success as an author. And, not to be forgotten, the money he received from these performances provided him with income when he most needed it.

4
Critical Analysis: Occasional Speeches

> [T]he orator should not be the leader of the multitude, but rather should be considered one of the multitude, deliberating with them upon common interests, which are well understood and valued by all."
>
> —Edward T. Channing

AFTER-DINNER SPEECHES

At a time when private societies of all sorts flourished, usually exclusive men's clubs, and their banquets abounded, the after-dinner speaker was much in demand. These banquets were usually multi-course feasts—extravagant meals accompanied with a surfeit of alcoholic drinks. The programs featured several speakers, sometimes as many as ten or twelve, who talked on various topics for various lengths of time. Conviviality was usually their purpose, and these orgies, as Twain described these rituals, lasted into the night. Of course, there were other dinners held for more purposeful reasons, where there was one speaker.

Because of his reputation as an entertainer, Mark Twain became the most-in-demand after-dinner speaker of his day. As his popularity rose, the speaking invitations multiplied to the point that he refused many and would show up only after the banquet for most.

On the whole, Twain's presentations were light and humorous, as the genre dictates, but he delivered some after-dinner speeches that were downright caustic. Three speeches relate directly to the genre: they address the need for speech-making reform. However, they vary in seriousness of purpose. "On Speech-Making Reform" presents a substantial lesson on effective speech-making, "Post-Prandial Oratory" entertains the audience with Twain's quick-fix solution to the problem of disappointing speech-making, and

"Dinner Speech" typifies the usual talk Twain presented at the many private dinners in his honor. These tended to be long on compliments and quick jokes and short on substance. "The Babies," more of a toast than a complete speech, is an especially excellent example of Twain's mastery of this genre. "Whittier's Birthday Speech," considered by some contemporaries as Twain's "hideous mistake," illustrates the particular demand that the after-dinner speech aim to promote the positive feelings of the audience. "Plymouth Rock and the Pilgrims" and "On Foreign Critics" stray from the prescribed mood of the genre. They are more diatribe than humorous discourse.

In general, Twain structured these speeches accordingly: He usually would begin with remarks about the chairman, the introduction, and members of the audience. After that, he usually stated the point he wished to make, presented some examples and stories loosely joined together, and concluded with another story or moral. Somehow, as rambling as his organization pattern seemed, he always came to a formidable conclusion.

"On Speech-Making Reform"

"On Speech-Making Reform" was delivered at the Tile Club Dinner for Lawrence Hutton in New York on March 31, 1885. The Tile Club was a group of artists who met in an old house on Tenth Street in New York. Laurence Hutton was an American essayist and critic and, relative to the topic, a noteworthy lecturer.

Twain begins with humorous remarks about his New Year's vow never to make another speech. Addressing the audience as "poor fellow sufferers, victims of the passion for speech-making," he inoculates his listeners with the mood of the moment and draws their attention to his topic—the need for speech-making reform. Although he treats this subject humorously, Twain, a serious student of the art of speech-making, aims to teach. His lesson is structured clearly: First, he states his definition of the expert speaker and follows with a descriptive example that apparently describes his style. With the phrase "[Y]ou can't reform that kind of man" as transition, Twain turns his attention to the "one sort that can be reformed . . . the genuinely impromptu speaker." Twain proceeds to describe this kind of speaker in the most humorous manner to the end of the speech.

The lesson begins with Twain's assertion that the art of public speaking requires study and practice: Successful orators "have learned their art by long observation and slowly compacted experience." Twain then explains that the effective speech is "not the actual impromptu one, but the counterfeit of it":

> [T]hat which has been carefully prepared in private and tried on a plaster cast, or an empty chair, or any other appreciative object that

> will keep quiet, until the speaker has got his matter and his delivery limbered up so that they will seem impromptu to an audience.

Twain also points out that the expert speaker prepares his speech by leaving "blanks here and there" where "genuine impromptu remarks can be dropped in, of a sort that will add to the natural aspect of the speech without breaking its line of march." The expert banquet speaker fills in these "blanks" with references to the speeches of the other speakers at a banquet.

Twain illustrates his point by detailing an example in which he shows the smoothness with which the expert speaker rises to the occasion. After complimenting the chairman and honored guests, he slides "into his set speech." "[Y]ou can't tell, to save you, where it was nor when it was that he made the connection." Then, almost lyrically, Twain describes the dynamic style of the veteran speaker:

> [He] will soar along, in the most beautiful way, on the wings of a practiced memory; heaving in a little decayed grammar here, and a little wise tautology there, and a little neatly counterfeited embarrassment yonder, and a little finely acted stumbling and stammering for a word—rejecting this word and that, and finally getting the right one, and fetching it out with ripping effect, and with the glad look of a man who has got out of a bad hobble entirely by accident, and wouldn't take a hundred dollars for that accident; and every now and then he will sprinkle you in one of those happy turns on something that has previously been said . . .

Finally, Twain describes the artistic mastery of the expert speaker's conclusion: On the act of sitting down, he will "lean over the table and fire a parting rocket, in the way of an afterthought, which makes everybody stretch his mouth as it goes up, and dims the very stars in heaven when it explodes." Twain reinforces his thesis by commenting that "that man has been practicing that afterthought and that attitude for about a week."

The speaker who needs reforming, according to Twain, is the man who "'didn't expect to be called upon, and isn't prepared'; and yet goes waddling and warbling along, just as if he thought it wasn't any harm to commit a crime so long as it wasn't premeditated." Twain demonstrates this speaker's calamity by imitating his attempts to get back to his seat. The speaker goes on and on. Twain explains in figurative terms:

> Now that man has no way of finding out how long his windmill is going. He likes to hear it creak; and so he goes on creaking . . . and when he comes to sit down at last, and look under his hopper, he is the most surprised person in the house to see what a little bit of grist

he has ground, and how unconscionably long he has been grinding it.

Twain summarizes this experience with his second main point of the lesson by stating that the speaker realizes that he "hasn't said anything—a discovery which the unprepared man ought usually to make, and does usually make—and has the added grief of making it at second hand, too."

Twain follows with another example of the speaker who needs reforming, the "man who provisions himself with a single prepared bite, of a sentence or two, and trusts to luck to catch quails and manna as he goes along." This kind of speaker sits smugly in his seat, contented with the belief that when he is introduced:

> [T]here is going to be such an electric explosion of applause that the inspiration of it will fill him instantly with ideas and clothe the ideas in brilliant language, and that an impromptu speech will result which will be infinitely finer than anything he could have deliberately prepared.

However, his unpreparedness creates the opposite effect. The reality is that he finds himself standing sick with apology. After stammering his few sentences, he "collapses into his seat, murmuring, 'I wish I was in,'—he doesn't say where." Although members of the audience mumble feeble compliments, the unprepared speaker is sick with embarrassment.

Twain teaches two facts about the unpredictability of the public speaking experience from this example: one, that the speaker never is called up when he thinks he will be, and that tends to cool his enthusiasm, and two, that repeating your short message over and over again will drain its credibility.

"Post-Prandial Oratory"

On October 20, 1887, at the Forefathers Day Dinner, Congregational Club, Music Hall, Boston, Twain again concerns himself with the common practice of after-dinner speaking. Similar to "On Speech-Making Reform," the objective of "Post-Prandial Oratory" is to make listeners aware of the importance of preparing speeches. However, the style of this work is more humorous than didactic. Twain's apparent intent is to entertain; however, it becomes clear through careful analysis of his method that his purpose is to teach. In this speech, Twain delivers his call for speech-making reform by obviously spoofing the attitude by some that speech-making is simple work.

Twain opens his humorous talk with the comment that "a public dinner is the most delightful thing in the world, to a guest" and that "a public dinner is the most unutterable suffering in the whole world, to a guest." With those statements, Twain immediately attracts the attention of his audience to his topic—the patent adjustable speech as a remedy to speaker unpreparedness.

Twain creates interest in his proposal by moving his audience to identify with the problem. Feigning great dramatic passion, he reviews the misery suffered by the many who were caught unprepared in a speaking situation. Then he clearly states his plan for no one ever to suffer such unpreparedness again:

> My scheme is this, that he shall carry in his head a cut-and-dried and thoroughly and glibly memorized speech that will fit every conceivable public occasion in this life, fit it to a dot, and win success and applause every time.

To prove that his patent adjustable speech can be used for any occasion, he develops his thesis by demonstrating how his system works. He explains that all one has to do is change three or four words in the content of the speech model and adjust the delivery according to the mood of the occasion.

With great fun, Twain instructs his listeners on how to use the patent adjustable speech for a granger meeting, a breakfast wedding, and a funeral. For example, he explains that after the person delivering the granger speech completes the usual introductory remarks and compliments, and just when he seems to be groping for words:

> [H]e opens his throttle valve and goes for those grangers. That person wants to be gorgeously eloquent; you want to fire the farmer's heart and start him from his mansard down to his cellar.

Twain advises that the breakfast speech be delivered in "an airy, light fashion, but it must terminate seriously." According to Twain, the patent adjustable speech lends itself best to the funeral. He demonstrates that it is a "most elastic speech" by showing how the substance can be adjusted according to the situation—for example, if the deceased is a wealthy cousin and "has remembered you in the will" or if the deceased left you "an ordinary horse." Revealing the anti-intellectualism of the self-made man, Twain quips, "A person can get so glib in a delivery of this speech, why by the time he has delivered it fifteen or twenty times he could go to any intellectual gathering in Boston even, and he would draw like a prizefight."

Twain concludes this speech by making fun of speech-making as he perceives it to exist in his time:

> The agricultural speech becomes a prohibition speech by putting in that word and changing 'economic' to moral, and 'physically' to morally. It becomes a Democratic, Republican, Mugwump or other

> political speech by shoving in the party name and changing 'economic' to political and 'physically' to politically.

Then he turns to his Boston audience with a playful jab: "Any of these forms can be used at a New England Forefathers dinner. *They* don't care what you talk about, so long as it ain't so."

"Dinner Speech" (Whitefriars Club)

At a dinner given in his honor by the Whitefriars Club, at the Hotel Cecil, London, June 16, 1899, Twain again relates to the subject of speech-making. The speech was a gala event with two hundred diners, including the American ambassador, Joseph H. Choate, and Senator Chauncey DePew, as well as a number of British dignitaries.

After a laudatory introduction, Twain greets his audience in his usual manner, with playful remarks relating to them. This time he kids the members of the Whitefriars Club about their title "Brethren of the Vow." Playing with the meaning of the word *vow*, Twain slips in a bit of moralizing by explaining: "A vow is always a pledge of some kind or other for the protection of your own morals and principles or somebody else's, and generally, by the irony of fate, it is for the protection of your own morals." He follows this teaching with a satirical comment about vow-making and human nature:

> Hence we have pledges that make us eschew tobacco or wine, and while you are taking the pledge there is a holy influence about that makes you feel you are reformed, and that you can never be so happy again in this world until—you get outside and take a drink.

Twain follows the acknowledgement of the organization with his usual comments about individual attenders. He recognizes George Augustus Sala, making lighthearted fun about Sala's public speaking. About his delivery, Twain jokes, "One did not need wine while he was making a speech. The rapidity of his utterance made a man drunk in a minute." He made fun of Sala's substance commenting, "He went into the whole history of the United States, and made it entirely new to me."

Finally, after being assured that he had the attention of his listeners, Twain makes specific reference to his topic: "I do not know anything so sad as a dinner where you are going to get up and say something by and by, and you do not know what it is." He lightly touches on the topic by citing the speaking talent of Ambassador Choate and Senator DePew, whom he referred to as "masters of oratory." Stating that from them he "learned to make after-dinner speeches," Twain discloses humorous recollections of their speaking experience.

He follows these appealing anecdotes with his usual commentary on the art of impromptu speaking. Then he launched into a long, hilarious story about a Doctor Hayes who learned too sadly about the pitfalls of preparing a speech in the manuscript mode.

Twain brings his discourse to a conclusion by calling attention to its obvious lack of substance: "I have been talking with so much levity that I have said no serious thing, and you are really no better or wiser." However, he turns this situation into a final compliment for this favored audience by referring to a member's comment that Twain is "a person who deals in wisdom." Therefore, Twain reasons, "I have said nothing which would make you better than when you came here." Then, since it is his custom to end with a maxim, some wise saying for them to take home as a "legacy" from him, he repeats his most often used aphorism: "'When in doubt, tell the truth.'"

"The Babies"

Following in the light-spirited tone that characterizes the after-dinner genre is Mark Twain's speech "The Babies. As They Comfort Us in Our Sorrows, Let Us Not Forget Them in Our Festivities." This piece of light satire was delivered as the final toast, the fifteenth, at the Thirteenth Reunion Banquet of the Army of the Tennessee, at the Palmer House, Chicago, November 13, 1879. Six hundred veterans, including generals Grant, Sherman, and Sheridan attended, and the patriotic festivities, including martial music and fireworks, went on almost all night. After an elaborate dinner, the speaking began with General Grant's toast at half past ten, "Our Country—Her Place among the Nations."

At three-thirty in the morning, Twain mounted the banquet table, gazed at the mighty generals, and raised his voice in salute to the babies: "We haven't all had the good fortune to be ladies; we haven't all been generals, or poets, or statesmen; but when the toast works down to the babies, we stand on common ground." With this statement, Twain states his rationale for the choice of subject. He also establishes the truth on which he logically builds his satire—the democratic ideal that all men are created equal.

His rhetoric is a masterful creation. With well-conceived logos, Twain constructs his commonsense argument that the baby is, indeed, the ultimate commander-in-chief. Therefore, the implication is that it is illogical to believe that one human can be superior to others. Twain uses the attenders' military experiences to promote identification. For example, he uses military terms to describe the arrival of a baby into one's life:

> You soldiers all know that when that little fellow arrived at family headquarters, you had to hand in your resignation. He took entire command. You became his lackey—his mere body servant, and you had to stand around, too. He was not a commander who made allowances for time, distance, weather, or anything else—you had to execute his order whether it was possible or not. And there was only one form of marching in his manual of tactics, and that was the double-quick. He treated you with every sort of insolence and disrespect, and the bravest of you didn't dare to say a word.

The most extraordinary feature of the work is the method Twain employs to effect humor. He uses the universally familiar behavior of babies and juxtaposes it with the image of the soldiers. The incongruous contrast makes for a most mirthful event. For example, Twain relates their heroic accomplishments in battle against the fiercest enemy to the subjugating power of the baby:

> You could face the death storm at Donelson and Vicksburg, and give back blow for blow; but when he clawed your whiskers, and pulled your hair, and twisted your nose, you had to take it. When the thunders of war were sounding in your ears, you set your face toward the batteries and advanced with steady tread; but, when he turned on the terrors of his war whoop, you advanced in the other direction—and mighty glad of the chance, too.

Twain's mood becomes serious as he turns to the conclusion. He speaks in exalting phrases about the baby's future, the future of America. Using the ship metaphor, which is common to a number of his speeches, Twain predicts that "our present schooner of State will have grown into a political leviathan—a *Great Eastern*—and the cradled babies of today will be on deck." He advises, "Let them be well trained, for we are going to leave a big contract on their hands."

However, in the following utterances, Twain is back to his usual playful self. Steadfast in his purpose, Twain talks of the future Admiral Farragut who at this moment is "*teething*—think of it!—and putting in a world of dead earnest, unarticulated and perfectly justifiable profanity over it, too."

Then, with the skill of the consummate craftsman, Twain effected a winning conclusion with a climax of comical images, including one of himself:

> And in still one more cradle, somewhere under the flag, the future illustrious Commander-in-Chief of the American armies is so little burdened with his approaching grandeurs and responsibilities as to be

> giving his whole strategic mind, at this moment, to trying to find out some way to get his own big toe into his mouth—an achievement which, meaning no disrespect, the illustrious guest of this evening turned *his* attention to some fifty-six years ago. And if the child is but a prophecy of the man, there are mighty few who will doubt that he *succeeded.*

Contemporary reports relate that "The Babies" was a huge success. The large banquet hall shook with constant laughter. Even the usually taciturn General Grant joined in.

"Dinner Speech" (Whittier's Birthday)

In contrast to "The Babies," which was predicated on total audience appeal and concluded with resounding acclamation, Twain's "Dinner Speech," on the occasion of the seventieth birthday of John Greenleaf Whittier, is considered his greatest fiasco. The banquet, organized by the publishers of the *Atlantic Monthly* to celebrate the twentieth anniversary of its founding, was held at the Hotel Brunswick, Boston, December 17, 1877. The speeches paid homage to the guest of honor and to all of the New England literary Brahmins assembled, including Ralph Waldo Emerson, Henry Wadsworth Longfellow, and Oliver Wendell Holmes. Twain was invited to speak by his good friend William Dean Howells, who assumed that such a performance might gain favor for Twain, still regarded in this company as a wild Westerner.

The problem with this speech, as a speech for oratorical study, is that Twain, quite uncharacteristically, seems unaware of his audience. His clear understanding of the relationship among the components of the speech event, speaker-message-audience, which he had heretofore effected so well, is not evident. On the surface, his purpose should have been concerned with impressing these literary giants who could further his career as a writer. That was his articulated career goal. Throughout his adult life, he spoke trivially of his performing talent, overtly dismissing it as simply a means to make quick money. When he suspected that his image as lecturer might cause him to be regarded as a "mere entertainer," he became depressed.

However, what is evident is Twain's actual motive for speaking as he did. Unconsciously, or perhaps consciously, Twain purposely chose the vernacular format and style of expression in order to fire yet another volley at his life-long foe—the dominant culture. The speech can be seen as an attempt by the American hero, in the name of the popular culture, to vanquish the foe. Twain's characterization of these literary giants functions as a leveling agent. His message is that of the self-made man asserting his equality to the intellectual elite.

This speech clearly indicates that Twain had made his choice to be true to his basic values. As much as Samuel L. Clemens strived for acceptance by the Eastern establishment, his public persona, and, as some scholars indicate, his alter ego, Mark Twain, preferred the West. This speech also reveals Twain as the Representative American, unrefined and out-of-touch with the mores of respectable society.

Howell's introduction, which later proved very ironic, of "a humorist who never makes you blush to have enjoyed his joke; whose generous wit has no meanness in it, whose fun is never at the cost of anything honestly high or good," was followed by Twain, the comic. Twain begins with an opening line reminiscent of the stock opening lines of today's comedians—"A funny thing happened on the way to the theater . . .": "Standing here on the shore of the Atlantic and contemplating certain of its biggest literary billows . . ." He then begins his burlesque in the frontier style of a "story within a story," a format he learned from his days in the Nevada Territory. Assuming the character of an old silver miner, Twain proceeds to lampoon all "littery" men by choosing the most revered—Whittier, Longfellow, Emerson, and Holmes—as his targets. He describes Emerson as "a seedy little bit of a chap," Holmes, as "fat as a balloon" with "double chins all the way down to his stomach," and Longfellow, as "built like a prizefighter. . . . His nose lay straight down his face, like a finger, with the end joint tilted up."

Uncharacteristically oblivious to audience feedback, Twain continued his "fun." He told the shocked audience: "They had been drinking—I could see that." Then he proceeded to parody their almost sacred works of poetry with the preface "And what queer talk they used." For example "Holmes," surveys the cabin and exclaims: "Build thee more stately mansions,/ O my Soul!" When "Longfellow" joins in with a misquote from *Hiawatha*, the miner interrupts with, "Begging your pardon, Mr. Longfellow, if you'll be so kind as to hold your yawp for about five minutes, and let me get this grub ready, you'll do me proud."

Although Twain concluded his speech by telling the miner that the drunks he met were not the literary giants but imposters, few in that gathering of prominent literati got the joke.

Perhaps the most interesting line, at least from the perspective of exploring motive, is in the conclusion. When Twain explains to the miner that those shiftless sorts were not the notable literary figures but imposters, Twain has the miner react: "Ah—imposters, were they?—are *you*?" Was Twain revealing self-doubt, his feeling that in this august assemblage *he* is the joke? The narration ends and Twain, the speaker, returns to the reality of the occasion and ends abruptly: "I did not pursue the subject; and since then I haven't traveled on my *nom de plume* enough to hurt."

Needless to say, many who heard or read about the speech, especially the reports of the event in the New England newspapers, were furious with Twain. They strongly criticized his irreverence. For over thirty years he reexamined the speech, vacillating between approval and disapproval. In 1906 he settled on approval, dismissing it as another chapter in "man's tragi-comic existence."[1]

All kinds of theories have been put forth as to why Twain made such a speech. Perhaps such a work resulted from Twain's natural impulsiveness: his belief that the humor of the hoax and the humor in the obvious incongruity of the situation would be clearly evident and overcome any hint of impropriety. Louis Budd interprets Twain's presentation as "aggression driven by self-hatred for courting the favor of New England."[2] Whatever the reason, the results tended to be overblown. The gentlemen who were burlesqued were relatively unaware of the furor. Emerson remained in a senile trance, but Whittier, Longfellow, and Holmes seemed somewhat amused. However, Twain agonized for months over what the newspapers claimed was an assault against good taste. After writing letters of apology to all involved, Twain wrote to stunned Howells in his inimitable style of combining pathos and humor: "Ah, well, I am a great and sublime fool. But then I am God's fool, and all his work must be contemplated with respect."[3]

"Plymouth Rock and the Pilgrims"

Four years later, on December 22, 1881, as guest speaker for the first annual dinner of the New England Society of Philadelphia, Twain delivered another attack on New England Brahmins. At the time "Plymouth Rock and the Pilgrims" was apparently accepted as typical Twainian humor, but under present-day scrutiny it is his most audacious criticism of the dominant culture.

In this address to the descendants of the *Mayflower*, Twain launches into a polemic, attacking the notions of superior ancestry held so sacredly by the members of his audience. He states his motive in the very first line: "I rise to protest." And protest he does, vehemently. Identifying with the popular culture struggling for respect, Twain boldly declares his superiority to the American Victorians:

> I am a border ruffian from the state of Missouri. I am a Connecticut Yankee by adoption. I have the morals of Missouri and the culture of Connecticut, and that's the combination that makes the perfect man.

Twain's argument is clear and relentless, initiated by his opening question: "Why do you want to celebrate *them* ['the *Mayflower* tribe'] for?" In forensic form, Twain sets out to destroy the credibility of the Pilgrim and, by doing so, those who honor their connection to them. First, he demeans the event: "[T]o be celebrating the mere landing of the Pilgrims . . . hang it, a horse would have known enough to land."

Second, Twain attacks the Pilgrims' revered reputation as founders of this nation of freedom. Stating his main point, "They took good care of themselves, but they abolished everybody else's ancestors," he proceeds to indict the Pilgrims for atrocious crimes against true Americans: "My first American ancestor, gentleman, was an Indian—an early Indian. Your ancestors skinned him alive, and I am an orphan." He accuses them of religious persecution of the Quakers and any other group that wished to practice freely: "Your ancestors—yes, they were a hard lot; but, nevertheless, they gave us religious liberty to worship as they required us to worship, and political liberty to vote as the church required."

Heightening his argument, Twain lists other crimes against his ancestors, such as the burning of the Salem witches and the introduction of slavery. At a time in our history when racial prejudice was particularly rampant, Twain brags about his relationship with the Negro slave: "I am of a mixed breed, an infinitely shaded and exquisite mongrel."

Always the moralizer, Twain scolds his audience about its appearance: "Cease to come to these annual orgies in this hollow modern mockery—the surplusage of raiment. Come in character." Implying that "clothes do not make the man," Twain refers to the Pilgrims' skinning of the Indian: [H]e was not a bird . . . he was a man."

In an effort to soften the effects of his message on the audience, and to remain within the parameters of the after-dinner speech, Twain assumed the persona of a fire and brimstone preacher and exhorted his listeners to reform:

> Disband these societies, hotbeds of vice, of moral decay—perpetuators of ancestral superstition. . . . renounce these soul-blistering saturnalia, cease from varnishing the rusty reputations of your long-vanished ancestors—the super-high moral old ironclads of Cape Cod, the pious buccaneers of Plymouth Rock—go home, and try to learn to behave!

Twain concludes his speech with a compliment about Pilgrim stock but then ends with a folksy zinger:

> People may talk as they like about that Pilgrim stock, but, after all's said and done, it would be pretty hard to improve on those people; and, as for me, I don't mind coming out flat-footed and saying there ain't any way to improve on them—except having them born in Missouri!

Obviously, Mark Twain took more risks as a speaker than as a writer. Evidence of his radical criticism of conventional society is not found in print until the publication of *Following the Equator* in 1897.

Because of his use of hyperbole and tongue-in-cheek delivery style, the "Plymouth Rock and the Pilgrims" speech was dismissed as a humorous presentation, too ludicrous to be taken seriously.

"On Foreign Critics"

Twain's after-dinner speech "On Foreign Critics," delivered in Boston on April 27, 1890, is far from humorous. In this speech, Twain dramatizes the fierce nationalistic spirit of the American. He presents a brilliant defense of American culture against the disparaging criticism of American civilization by some Europeans. Specifically, Twain addresses the comments that the British critic Matthew Arnold made in his essays published in the *Nineteenth Century*: "A Word about America" (May, 1882), "A Word More about America" (February, 1885), and "Civilisation in the United States" (April, 1888), and during his lecture tour in the United States, 1883-84.

Twain responded for both patriotic and personal reasons. Outwardly, he was provoked by Arnold's repeated affirmation of the abusive opinions of American life as described by the British nobleman Sir Lepel Henry Griffin in his book *The Great Republic*. Published in New York and London and later reprinted in parts in the *Fortnightly Review* for January and March, 1884, Lepel characterizes the United States accordingly:

> America of to-day, the apotheosis of Philistinism . . . the Mecca to which turns every religious or social charlatan, where the only god worshipped is Mammon . . . where political life . . . is shunned by an honest man as the plague; where, to enrich jobbers and monopolists and contractors, a nation has emancipated its slaves and enslaved its freemen, where the people is gorged and drunk with materialism, and where wealth has become a curse instead of a blessing. . . . With some experience of every country in the civilised world, I can think of none except Russia in which I would not prefer to reside, in which life would not be more worth living, less sordid and mean and unlovely.[4]

Inwardly, Twain had a personal grievance. Arnold was a guest in Twain's home in Hartford in 1883, and hardly five years later, in his essay "Civilisation in the United States," Arnold cites Twain's popularity as a writer to support his argument that American civilization is so substandard: Arnold argues that a chief reason why American civilization is so lacking is because of the "addiction to 'the funny man,' who is a national misfortune there." Americans are middle-class Philistines, Arnold asserts, for Mark Twain could please only shallow-minded Philistines, being a writer of false literature delighted in by childish and half-savage minds.

In "On Foreign Critics," Twain demonstrates his rhetorical mastery. His intent is to refute such criticism by proving that the American nation is the only "real" civilization. First, he dismisses all attempts to denotatively define *civilization* as inadequate—"Nobody can answer that conundrum. They have all tried." Instead, he chooses to present his argument inductively with the explication of the question: "What is a 'real' civilization?" Twain builds his case to prove, without question, that the American civilization is the only "real" civilization because it is based upon human liberty.

Twain presents his rhetorical strategy with typical American common sense. First, he addresses the two questions which have to first be resolved: "What is a 'real' civilization?" and "How old is real civilization?" For the first question, Twain reasons that since there is no acceptable definition of a "real" civilization, "suppose we try to get at what it is not; and then subtract the what it is not from the general sum, and call the remainder 'real' civilization." Therefore, he posits a working definition:

> Any system which has in it any one of these things, to wit, human slavery, despotic government, inequality, numerous and brutal punishments for crimes, superstition almost universal, ignorance almost universal, and dirt and poverty almost universal—is not a real civilization, and any system which has none of them, is.

For the second question, he reasons:

> [S]ince civilization must surely mean the humanizing of a people, not a class—there is today but one real civilization in the world, and it is not yet thirty years old. We made the trip and hoisted its flag when we disposed of our slavery.

Then he presents his evidence by examining so-called civilizations and denouncing them. For example, he removes the French from contention by explaining that they "were a starving nation clothed in rags, slaves of an aristocracy of smirking dandies clad in unearned silks and velvet" before the American Revolution happened to change the course of their lives. Comments Twain, "It makes one's cheek burn to read of the laws of the time and realize that they were for human beings; realize that they originated in this world, and not in hell." He characterizes Germany as "unspeakable." And he stomps Great Britain's chances by describing the squalid living conditions of the poor:

> In England there was a sham liberty, and not much of that; crime was general; ignorance the same; poverty and misery were widespread; London fed a tenth of her population by charity; the law awarded the death penalty to almost every conceivable offense; what was called medical science by courtesy stood where it had stood for two thousand years; Tom Jones and Squire Western were gentlemen.

Then Twain used what he believed to be the guardian of truth and justice, the newspaper, to further castigate his adversaries and champion his cause. He accused Germany, France, and England of having the printer's art for centuries, but "In all that time there has not been a newspaper in Europe that was worthy the name." Twain charges, "When we hoisted the banner of revolution and raised the first genuine shout for human liberty that had ever been heard, this was a newspaperless globe."

In a rousing summation of his argument, Twain declares:

> Who woke that printing press out of its trance of three hundred years? Let us be permitted to consider that we did it. Who summoned the French slaves to rise and set the nation free? We did it. What resulted in England and on the Continent? Crippled liberty took up its bed and walked. From that day to this its march has not halted, and please God it never will. We are called the nation of inventors. And we are. We could still claim that title and wear its loftiest honors, if we had stopped with the first thing we ever invented—which was human liberty. Out of that invention has come the Christian world's great civilization. Without it it was impossible—as the history of all the centuries has proved. Well, then, who invented civilization? Even Sir Lepel Griffin ought to be able to answer that question. It looks easy enough. *We* have contributed nothing! Nothing hurts me like ingratitude.

Then Twain, Representative American, protagonist for the popular culture, with great eloquence and characteristic common sense, confronts Matthew Arnold's charge that the American society "seems organized" for the benefit of "that immense class, the great bulk of the community":

> Mr. Arnold's indicated civilization would seem to be restricted, by its narrow lines and difficult requirements, to a class—the top class—as in tropical countries snow is restricted to the mountain summits. . . . The impression you get of it is, that it is peculiarly hard, and

glittering, and bloodless, and unattainable. Now if our bastard were a civilization, it could fairly be figured—by Mr. Arnold's own concessions—by the circulation of the blood, which nourishes and refreshes the whole body alike, delivering its rich streams of life and health impartially to the imperial brain and the meanest extremity.

"On Foreign Critics" is a brilliant polemic. Unfortunately, Matthew Arnold did not hear about it, for he died shortly before the event. Nevertheless, the message went forth to all who touted the superiority of other cultures over that of America.

It should be noted here that Twain attacked Matthew Arnold on an earlier occasion. Three years earlier, on coincidentally the same date, April 27, 1887, Twain addressed the Ninth Annual Reunion Banquet at the Army and Navy Club of Connecticut in Central Hall, Hartford. This rather brief, but bellicose speech expresses the indignation of patriotic Americans who protested Arnold's criticism of General Grant's command of the English language in his review of Grant's *Memoirs*.[5]

OCCASIONAL SPEECHES

Twain's speeches classified as "occasional" refer to those discourses that address topics appropriate to the time and the place of the gathering. The arrangement of such presentations, in general, were similar to that of the after-dinner speeches: an opening reference to the chairman, members of the audience, and the occasion; a statement of thesis, followed by a topical or rambling development of supporting material, culminating in a return to his thesis; and a satisfying memorable statement. Examples of such speeches are a typical satirical piece, "Advice to Youth," three uncharacteristically serious political diatribes—one addressing municipal corruption, "Edmund Burke on Croker and Tammany," and two attacking the policy of imperialism, "Remarks" and "Introducing Winston S. Churchill" and two eloquent ceremonial speeches, "Our Guest" and his "Seventieth Birthday Speech."

"Advice to Youth"

"Advice to Youth," a speech delivered to the Saturday Morning Club in Boston on April 15, 1882, is a classic example of Twain's typical speaking style—the use of satirical humor for rhetorical purposes. As usual, his target was the dominant culture. In this speech to a group of young people, Twain criticizes the high moral tone of some of their educational precepts and the precepts themselves. He develops the satire by reciting maxims regarding conventional behavior. After each statement, he utters a more realistic comment. Although this style is obviously humorous, Twain's message is for youth to question the logic of such rules. His motive is to teach his young listeners to think on their own, to be responsible for their own actions:

> Always obey you parents, when they are present. . . . Be respectful to your superiors, if you have any . . . If a person offend you, and you are in doubt as to whether it was intentional or not, do not resort to extreme measures; simply watch your chance and hit him with a brick. . . . If you shall find that he has not intended any offense, come out frankly and confess yourself in the wrong when you struck him; acknowledge it like a man and say you didn't mean to. Yes, always avoid violence; in this age of charity and kindliness, the time has gone by for such things. Leave dynamite to the low and unrefined.

Twain, often referred to as the Moralist of the Main, points out the moral hypocrisy governing why it is wrong to lie: "You want to be very careful about lying; otherwise you are nearly sure to get caught." He continues, sarcastically: "For the history of our race, and each individual's experience, are sown thick with evidence that a truth is not hard to kill, and that a lie well told is immortal."

Twain concludes his moral lesson with a poke at conformity:

> Build your character thoughtfully and painstakingly upon these precepts; and by and by, when you have got it built, you will be surprised and gratified to see how nicely and sharply it resembles everybody else's.

Mark Twain's view of America at the dawn of the twentieth century was one of much disappointment, causing him to lament that this new era was not his. The Gilded Age, as he termed it, was morally corrupt. He was angry with the politics and the politicians for their blatant exploitation of human beings, and he used the speaker's platform to express boldly his fury. These speeches are serious and deliberate, with no indication of Twain the humorist. With "Edmund Burke on Croker and Tammany," Twain effectively attacks corrupt municipal government. Two rather brief but potent diatribes, "Remarks" and "Introducing Winston S. Churchill," take on governments, foreign and domestic, who practiced imperialism.

"Edmund Burke on Croker and Tammany"

"Edmund Burke on Croker and Tammany" was presented at a dinner of the Order of the Acorns, an organization of newspapermen principally, at the Waldorf-Astoria Hotel in New York City on October 17, 1901. It is a masterful polemic indicting Richard Croker and his political organization, Tammany Hall, of corruption. Carefully constructed in the manuscript mode, this speech demonstrates Twain's mastery of deliberative rhetoric. He argues his case against Croker by demonstrating the parallel between the impeachment argument of the brilliant British parliamentary orator Edmund Burke against the corrupt Warren Hastings of the East India Company. Twain's clever method of development to achieve closure with this favorable and influential audience is that of replicating Burke's speech with appropriate adjustments. He prefaces each excerpt of Burke's points by noting such changes: For example, "In the following, let 'persons' stand for 'Tammany.' For 'India' read 'Tammany.' For 'Parliament' read 'parties.' For 'nation' read 'city.' For 'India' read 'New York'." Twain concludes his speech with his adaptation of Burke's climactic peroration:

> [T]o the voters of New York . . . "it is with confidence that, ordered by the people—
>
> "I impeach Richard Croker of high crimes and misdemeanors.
>
> "I impeach him in the name of the people, whose trust he has betrayed.
>
> "I impeach him in the name of all the people of America, whose national character he has dishonored.
>
> "I impeach him in the name and by virtue of those eternal laws ofjustice which he has violated.
>
> "I impeach him in the name of human nature itself, which he has cruelly outraged, injured, and oppressed, *in both sexes, in every age, rank, situation, and condition of life.*

Like his prototype Edmund Burke, Mark Twain was successful. The speech was reprinted, and thousands of copies were distributed. In the municipal election that November, Richard Croker and his corrupt political machine, Tammany Hall, were voted out of power.

Always the defender of human rights and the foe of hypocrisy, Twain risked his popular status by lashing out against imperialistic practices. He wrote four potent speeches on the issue; three were delivered, and the fourth, which reached the greatest audience, was printed. Many who heard or read them were shocked, not only because of his message but also because it was not in character with the man they knew and loved. Some newspapers even used the term "traitor" to refer to the gentleman renown as the Representative American.

"Remarks" (Public Education Association)

The first of Twain's anti-imperialist speeches, "Remarks," was an address to the Public Education Association of New York City at the Berkeley Lyceum on November 23, 1900. Approximately 700 women attended. They were members of this humanitarian organization that fostered public education, particularly in the slums of New York's East Side.

After complimenting his audience on their good work, Twain refers to the fact that photographs of the New York schools have been sent throughout Europe as models for foreign governments and that they are currently in Russia. And, amazes Twain, at the same time, news from Russia is that it proposes to retrench from its incursion into Manchuria. From that statement of fact, Twain launches his attack on all imperialist nations: "If Russia retrenches this way why shouldn't Germany and France follow suit?" His questioning focuses on China: "Why should not China be free from the foreigners?" Twain directs his anger toward Western imperialism in China, attacking American policy as hypocritical:

> As far as America is concerned we don't allow the Chinese to come here, and we would be doing the graceful thing to allow China to decide whether she will allow us to go there. China never wanted any foreigners, and when it comes to a settlement of the immigrant question I am with the Boxer every time.[6]
>
> The Boxer is a patriot; he is the only patriot China has. The Boxer believes in driving us out of his country. I wish him success.

After this brief tirade, Twain returns to his topic—the importance of public education: "It occurred to me to finish that cablegram. The rest said: 'Russia, in order to retrench, has resolved to withdraw the appropriation for public schools.'" He concludes his remarks with some folksy wisdom about taking money from public education: "It's like feeding a dog on his own tail. It wouldn't fatten that dog."

Twain concludes this brief speech with a rather sober statement: "This society is much wiser in its day and generation than the Emperor of Russia and all his people. That is not much of a compliment, but it's the best I've got in stock."

"Introducing Winston S. Churchill"

Twain's second anti-imperialism speech, "Introducing Winston S. Churchill," was presented a month after the first. He was chosen to introduce the young hero of the Boer War, who was sent to the United States to promote Anglo-American unity. The "fashionable audience" assembled in the Grand Ballroom of the Waldorf-Astoria Hotel in New York on December 12, 1900.

Twain begins the address by bluntly stating: "Mr. Churchill and I do not agree on the righteousness of the South African War." Referring to himself as a "self-appointed missionary," Twain proceeds to accuse England of having "sinned" for fighting the Boer War and the United States for fighting the Spanish-American War. For England, "mother of human liberty," and America, "the refuge of the homeless, the hunted, the oppressed from everywhere," to loot other nations for selfish gains is most hypocritical. Twain concludes by referring to the kinship between England and America:

> [K]in blood, kin in religion, kin in representative government, kin in ideals, kin in just and lofty purposes; and now we are kin in sin, the harmony is complete, the blend is perfect.

The printed speech, termed a "salutation-speech" by Twain, briefly and blatantly states his feelings about events in the new century:

> A Salutation-Speech from the 19th Century to the 20th, taken down in shorthand by Mark Twain: I bring you the stately matron named Christendom, returning bedraggled, besmirched & dishonored from pirate-raids in Kiao-Chouw, Manchuria, South Africa & the Philippines, with her soul full of meanness, her pocket full of boodle, & her mouth full of pious hypocrisies. Give her soap & a towel, but hide the looking glass.[7]

Composed a few days after the public education speech in which he declared the rebellious Boxers of China as patriots, the speech was obviously an act of defiance to his detractors. It was printed in the *New York Herald* on December 30, 1900, and widely distributed.[8] Reactions included the commentary in the *Nation*, which tended to dismiss Twain's condemnation by referring to him as this "old-fashioned American."[9]

"Our Guest" (Lord Mayor's Banquet)

Although Twain chastised Britain for its imperialistic ways, he, indeed, felt a powerful kinship for the English, and the feeling was more than mutual. No speech exemplifies this strong bond more than "Our Guest." Delivered at the Lord Mayor's Banquet for Twain in Town Hall in Liverpool, England, on July 10, 1907, it was one in a series of banquets feting Twain's honorary doctorate from Oxford University. Twain was seventy-two years old and he knew this would be his last trip to England. Several hundred people attended the feast, and after the second toast to "Our Guest," Twain addressed his admirers with a skillful mix of humor and pathos.

The speech reflects his usual after-dinner style, but it is special. After his usual run of funny comments and stories, Twain's tone becomes serious. Labeling himself an Ambassador, he speaks warmly of the strong connections between America and Britain. And then, in almost solemn tones, he expresses his gratitude to Oxford for having conferred on him "the loftiest honor that has ever fallen to my fortune" and to all those who have honored him during his four-week stay. He recalls their gesture of affection: "[T]he hearty hand grip and the cordial welcome which does not descend from the pale grey matter of the brain, but comes up with the red blood out of the heart."

The eloquent conclusion makes this speech particularly extraordinary. Twain expresses his farewell by referring to a passage from the British author Dana's book *Two Years Before the Mast*. Using the ship metaphor, the wistful Mississippi Pilot illustrates how the British have made him feel:

> During perhaps one hour in the twenty-four—not more than that—I stop and reflect. Then I am humble, then I am properly meek, and for that little time I am "only the *Mary Ann*," fourteen hours out, and cargoes with vegetables and tinware; but all the other twenty-three my vain self-satisfaction rides high and I am the stately Indiaman, plowing the great seas under a cloud of sail, and laden with a rich freightage of the kindest words that were ever spoken to a wandering alien, I think; my twenty-six crowded and fortunate days seem multiplied by five, and I am the *Begum of Bengal*, a hundred and twenty-three days out from Canton—homeward bound!

As Charles Vale wrote in *The Forum*: "Only a great litterateur could have conceived such a passage: only a great orator could have so delivered it."[10]

"Dinner Speech" (Seventieth Birthday)

"Dinner Speech," presented on the occasion of his seventieth birthday, is considered his best by some. For this special event Twain emerged from retirement after the death of his wife in June 1904. Held on December 5, 1905, at Delmonico's in New York City, the celebration was attended by a crowd of prominent citizens, including more than sixty women. It was a grand celebration, complete with a forty-piece orchestra playing background music. William Dean Howells, the toastmaster, introduced Twain by reading a twenty-eight-line poem that defined the American joke:

I jolly the whole earth,
But most I love to jolly my own kind,
Joke of a people great, gay, bold, and free,
I type their master-mood, Mark Twain made me.

Howells then hailed the guest of honor: "I will not say, 'Oh King, live forever,' but 'Oh King, live as long as you like!'"[11]

Twain addressed the occasion by presenting a wise, yet humorous, lesson on growing old. He used his inimitable humorous style to communicate the virtues of authenticity and autonomy.

The chief part of his speech is a discussion of the maxim: "We can't reach old age by another man's road." Declaring, "I am here to teach," Twain illustrates the truth of that statement by reviewing his own lifestyle. In a clear, topical pattern, the master humorist assesses his habits concerning sleeping, eating, smoking, drinking, and exercising in his delightful, inimitable style. For example, about his love of smoking, he jokes, "[I]t has always been my rule never to smoke when asleep, and never to refrain when awake." Then he instructs: "It is a good rule, I mean, for me; but some of you know quite well that it wouldn't answer for everybody that's trying to get to be seventy." After this instruction, he repeats his thesis warning: "My habits protect my life but they would assassinate you." Simply stated, his message is to be true to ourselves, for we are individuals.

Toward the end of the speech, Twain amuses the audience by addressing his favorite topic for satire: morals. By talking about morals as if they were some tangible entity, he lampoons the behavior of the self-righteous. "Morals are an acquirement—like music, like a foreign language, like piety, poker, paralysis—no man is born with them," Twain jokes irreverently. With light-hearted sarcasm and the vernacular style, he talks about his "old secondhand moral, all out of repair, and didn't fit, anyway" and how one should "be careful with a thing like that." If you give it "a fresh coat of whitewash once in a while . . . she will keep sweet, or at least inoffensive." He talks about working "her Sundays." After she lost her character from associating with insurance presidents, he sold her to King Leopold of Belgium. This absurd, obviously false account serves to expose society's ridiculous preoccupation with *possessing* morals.

Twain concludes this discourse by returning to the rhetorical situation—his seventieth birthday. Since seventy is "the Scriptural statute of limitations," he reasons that a person no longer has to work. Then, with an affectionate tone, he bids his public farewell. His final statement, like that of the "Lord Mayor's Dinner," uses the metaphor of the ship to wish all well on their life's journey:

> Your invitation honors me, and pleases me because you will keep me in your remembrance, but I am seventy; seventy, and would nestle in the chimney corner, and smoke my pipe, and read my book, and take my rest, wishing you well in all affection, and that when you in your turn shall arrive at pier No. 70 you may step aboard your waiting ship with a reconciled spirit, and lay your course toward the sinking sun with a contented heart.

Twain's use of the ship metaphor seems to indicate his sense of individualism. We are all pilots of our own ships, with the free will to chart our own courses.

Twain's speeches, almost two hundred of them, cover a variety of subjects in an assortment of styles. However, his motives for speaking remained constant.

Mark Twain with Twain family employee, John Lewis, 1903. Mark Twain Memorial, Hartford, CT.

5
Epilogue

Charles Vale, in his article "Mark Twain As An Orator," written in *The Forum* in 1910, summarized Twain's speaking career:

> Mark Twain personified the most valuable and obvious traits of the American character—the ability and the desire for hard work; contempt for the finicking, the insincere, the affected; bitter scorn for the larger shams of the unit and the multitude—graft, greed, hypocrisy, cant. In a land of vast possibilities, but some unpleasant realities, he upheld the banner of commercial integrity and maintained the moral obligation of every man to pay his debts in full—as Nature pays hers. . . . For Mark Twain was an orator, and not merely a molder of evanescent epigrams. His grip—the grip of a controller of men—was upon all who watched, and listened, and wondered; and slowly, quietly, he showed them what few, perhaps, had suspected—the large emotions of one who has lived, suffered, worked, thought and remembered. None would accuse him of sentimentality: he never cultivated the tricks of the mere showman, or sought refuge in the facile revelations of the self-pitier. But just as he represented the obvious traits of the typical American character—sincerity in word and deed—so also he represented the unobvious, and sometimes unsuspected, traits—the emotional susceptibility, the questioning for the ideal, all the spiritual unrest and human lovableness lying deep, very deep, in the heart of the race which is outwardly brusque and business-like to the point of brutality and offensive rudeness.[1]

Twain made speeches for all sorts of occasions to all kinds of audiences. They ran the gamut of emotions, from lighthearted humor to biting sarcasm to warm affection. Although his messages may be regarded as more reactive than proactive, they were effective. Twain, the man, benefitted because these social interactions defined his character; Twain, the artist, gained because the platform experience developed his craft. The nation and the world profited because they learned to respect the promises of democracy. And, we, the human being, advanced because we were gifted with his model.

Notes

CHAPTER 1: MARK TWAIN: A GREAT AMERICAN ORATOR

1. See Louis J. Budd, *Our Mark Twain: The Making of His Public Personality* (Philadelphia: University of Pennsylvania Press, 1983), 171.

2. Samuel L. Clemens, *Mark Twain's Speeches with an Introduction by Albert Bigelow Paine and an Appreciation by William Dean Howells* (New York: Harper and Brothers Publishers, 1923), xiv.

3. Alan Gribben, "The Importance of Mark Twain," *American Quarterly* 37 (1986): 57.

4. Budd, 57.

5. Budd, 58.

6. Budd, 57.

7. See an analysis of this speech in Chapter 3 of this volume; the text can be found in Part II.

8. Robert M. Rodney and Minnie M. Brashear, *The Art, Humor, and Humanity of Twain* (Norman, Okla.: University of Oklahoma Press, 1960), vii.

9. Bernard DeVoto, ed., *Mark Twain in Eruption: Hitherto Unpublished Pages about Man and Events by Mark Twain* (New York: Harper and Brothers, 1922), 202.

10. DeVoto, 202.

11. DeVoto, 202.

12. Frederick J. Antczak, *Thought and Character: The Rhetoric of Democratic Education* (Ames: The Iowa State University Press, 1985).

13. Clemens.

14. Paul Fatout, ed., *Mark Twain Speaking* (Iowa City: University of Iowa Press, 1976).

15. Fatout, xxx.

16. Fatout, xxx.

17. Albert Bigelow Paine, ed., *Mark Twain's Letters*, 2 vols. (New York: Harper and Brothers Publishers, 1917), 1: 59.

18. See Introduction by W.D. Howells in Samuel L. Clemens, *Mark Twain's Speeches* (New York: Harper and Brothers, 1910).

19. Fatout, xxx.

20. Dixon Wecter, ed., *The Love Letters of Mark Twain* (New York: Harper and Brothers, 1949), 116.

21. Wecter, 116.

22. Wecter, 116.

23. Wecter, 117.

24. An analysis of this speech is in Chapter 4 of this volume; the text is in Part II.

25. Samuel L. Clemens, *Literary Essays* (New York: Harper and Brothers, 1918).

26. Marlene Boyd Vallin, "Mark Twain, Platform Artist: A Nineteenth-Century Preview of Twentieth-Century Performance Theory, *Text and Performance Quarterly* 9 (1989): 322-333.

27. Marlene Boyd Vallin, "'Manner Is Everything': The Secret to Mark Twain's Performing Success," *Journal of Popular Culture* 24 (1990): 81-90.

28. Daniel J. Boorstin, *The Americans: The National Experience* (New York: Random House, 1966), 323.

29. Charles Wagenknecht, *Mark Twain: The Man and His World* (New York: Yale University Press, 1940), 93.

30. Boorstin, 312. Eugene Bahn and Margaret L. Bahn, *A History of Oral Interpretation* (Minneapolis: Burgess Publishing Co., 1970), 155.

31. Karl R. Wallace, ed., *History of Speech Education in America* (New York: Appleton-Century-Crofts, Inc., 1954), 108.

32. Antczak, 130.

33. Hitherto Unpublished Letter to W.D. Howells, November 17, 1879.

34. DeVoto, 216.

35. Henry Nash Smith, *Mark Twain: The Development of a Writer* (Cambridge, Mass.: The Belknap Press of Harvard University Press, 1962), vii.

36. Charles Miner Thompson, "Mark Twain as an Interpreter of American Character," *Atlantic Monthly* 79 (April 1897): 450.

37. Antczak, 222.

38. Louis J. Budd, "Hiding Out in Public: Mark Twain as a Speaker," *Studies in American Fiction* 13 (Autumn 1986): 137.

39. Gribben, 45.

40. Budd, 241.

CHAPTER 2: RHETORICAL APPRAISAL

1. Wayne C. Booth, "The Rhetorical Stance," *College Composition and Communication* XIV (October 1963): 139-145.

2. Albert Bigelow Paine, ed., *Mark Twain's Letters*, 2 vols. (New York: Harper and Brothers, 1912), 2: 449.

3. Dixon Wecter, ed., *The Love Letters of Mark Twain* (New York: Harper and Brothers, 1949), 162.

4. Bernard DeVoto, ed., *Mark Twain in Eruption: Hitherto Unpublished Pages about Man and Events by Mark Twain* (New York: Harper and Brothers, 1922), 202.

5. Henry Steel Commager, *The American Mind: An Interpretation of American Thought and Character Since the 1880's* (New Haven: Yale University Press, 1950).

6. Commager, 13.

7. Commager, 25.

8. Commager, 24.

9. See Marlene Boyd Vallin, "Mark Twain, Platform Performer: A Nineteenth-Century Preview of Twentieth-Century Performance Theory, *Text and Performance Quarterly* 9 (1989): 322-323.

10. Paine, 2: 542.

11. Fred W. Lorch, *The Trouble Begins at Eight: Mark Twain's Lecture Tours* (Ames: Iowa State University Press, 1968), 212.

12. William Dean Howells, *My Mark Twain: Reminiscences and Criticisms* (Baton Rouge: Louisiana State University Press, 1910), 44.

13. Kenneth Burke, *A Grammar of Motives and A Rhetoric of Motives* (Cleveland, Ohio: The World Publishing Co., 1962), 579.

14. Samuel Clemens, *Mark Twain's Speeches with an Introduction by Albert Bigelow Paine and an Appreciation by William Dean Howells* (New York: Harper and Brothers Publishers, 1923), xiv.

15. Lloyd F. Bitzer, "The Rhetorical Situation," *Philosophy and Rhetoric* 1 (1968): 1-15.

16. Paine, 2: 527-528.

17. Paul Fatout, ed., *Mark Twain Speaking* (Iowa City: University of Iowa Press, 1976), 179-180.

18. See a critical analysis of this speech in Chapter 4 of this volume; the text is in Part II.

19. Fatout, 576.

20. Burke, 570.

21. "Mark Twain At Home, An Anti-Imperialist," *New York Herald* 16 October 1900: 4.

22. Henry Nash Smith, *Mark Twain: The Development of a Writer*

(Cambridge, Mass.: Belknap Press of Harvard University Press, 1962), 106.

23. Louis J. Budd, *Our Mark Twain: The Making of His Public Personality* (Philadelphia: University of Pennsylvania Press, 1983), 25.

24. See a critical analysis of this lecture in Chapter 3 of this volume; the text is in Part II.

25. See a critical analysis of this speech in Chapter 4 of this volume; the text is in Part II.

26. All these speeches are analyzed in Chapters 3 and 4 of this volume; their texts are in Part II.

27. See a critical analysis of this lecture in Chapter 3 of this volume; the text is in Part II.

28. Walter Blair, *Horse Sense in American Humor* (New York: Russell and Russell, 1942), v.

29. Lorch, 212.

30. Howells, 44.

31. *New York Herald*, 7 May 1867: 4.

32. Archibald Henderson, *Mark Twain* (New York: F.A. Stokes, 1910), vii.

33. "Mark Twain on the Platform," *The Critic* (April 25, 1896): 2.

34. See Clemens, xiv.

35. DeVoto, 224.

36. DeVoto, 225.

37. See Twain's essay "How to Tell a Story," in Samuel L. Clemens, *Literary Essays* (New York: Harper and Brothers, 1918), 9.

38. George Hiram Brownell, ed., *Revived Remarks on Mark Twain by George Ade* (Chicago: Privately printed, 1936), 10.

39. Fatout, 250.

40. Edwin Black, "The Second Persona," *Quarterly Journal of Speech* 56 (April 1970): 119.

41. Howells, 5.

42. DeVoto, 217.

43. "Mark Twain on the Platform," *The Critic*, 296.

44. Clemens, xiv.

45. Mark Twain's Notebooks, *The Mark Twain Papers* (University of California Library, Berkeley) SLC to OLC, 15 January 1870.

46. Budd, 7.

47. Louis J. Budd, *Critical Essays on Mark Twain, 1867-1910* (Boston, Mass.: G.K. Hall and Co., 1982), 8.

48. Gamaliel Bradford, *American Portraits* (Boston and New York: Houghton Mifflin Co., 1922), 4.

49. Richard Weaver, *Ethics of Rhetoric* (Chicago: Henry Regnery Company, 1970), 16.

CHAPTER 3: CRITICAL ANALYSIS: LECTURES

1. J.G. Holland, "The Popular Lecture," *Atlantic Monthly* 15 (March 1865): 363.

2. Louis J. Budd, in *Our Mark Twain: The Making of His Public Personality* (Philadelphia: University of Pennsylvania Press, 1983), 131, remarks that "[s]ome of Twain's serious oratory was 'literature' and would still qualify if notions of genre had not narrowed."

3. Fred W. Lorch, *The Trouble Begins at Eight: Mark Twain's Lecture Tours* (Ames: Iowa State University Press, 1966), 31.

4. In *Roughing It*, Chapter LXXVI, Twain describes this experience with embellishments.

5. "Mark Twain's Lecture," *New York Times*, 7 May 67: 5.

6. "Mark Twain at the Cooper Institute," *New York Herald*, 7 May 67: 4.

7. Anonymous, Reprinted from *Spectator* [London] 46 (October 18, 1873): 1302-1303.

8. Dixon Wecter, ed., *Mark Twain to Mrs. Fairbanks* (San Marino, Cal.: Huntington Library, 1949), 44.

9. Wecter, 158. Lorch devotes a whole chapter in *The Trouble Begins at Eight* to this experience: Chapter 9, "The Most Detestable Campaign."

10. Albert Bigelow Paine, ed., *Mark Twain's Letters*, 2 vols. (New York: Harper and Row, Publishers, 1917), 1: 193.

11. Lorch, 321.

CHAPTER 4: CRITICAL ANALYSIS: OCCASIONAL SPEECHES

1. For a thorough account of this event, see Henry Nash Smith's "That Hideous Mistake of Poor Clemens's," *Harvard Library Bulletin* 9 (Spring 1955): 145-180.

2. Louis J. Budd, *Our Mark Twain: The Making of His Public Personality* (Philadelphia: University of Pennsylvania Press, 1983), 59.

3. Albert Bigelow Paine, ed., *Mark Twain's Letters,* 2 vols. (New York: Harper and Brothers Publishers, 1917) 1: 317-318.

4. See D.M. McKeithan, "The Occasion of Mark Twain's Speech on Foreign Critics," *Philogical Quarterly* 28 (July 1948): 276-279.

5. See Paul Fatout, ed., *Mark Twain Speaking* (Iowa City: University of Iowa Press, 1976), 225-227.

6. In 1900, the "Boxers," a Chinese patriotic secret society, attacked the foreigners in China, murdering more than three hundred. An international army, including American soldiers, rescued the remaining Europeans and put

down the rebellion.

7. Budd, 172.
8. Budd, 173.
9. Budd, 173.
10. Charles Vale, "Mark Twain as an Orator," *The Forum* 44 (July 1910): 4.
11. Fatout, 462.

CHAPTER 5: EPILOGUE

1. Charles Vale, "Mark Twain as an Orator," *The Forum* 44 (July 1910): 2-3.

II
COLLECTED SPEECHES

"Sandwich Islands Lecture"

Ladies and gentlemen: The next lecture in this course will be delivered this evening by Samuel L. Clemens, a gentleman whose high character and unimpeachable integrity are only equalled by his comeliness of person and grace of manner. And I am the man! I was obliged to excuse the chairman from introducing me, because he never compliments anybody and I knew I could do it just as well.

The Sandwich Islands will be the subject of my lecture—when I get to it—and I shall endeavor to tell the truth as nearly as a newspaper man can. If I embellish it with a little nonsense, that makes no difference; it won't mar the truth; it is only as the barnacle ornaments the oyster by sticking to it. That figure is original with me! I was born back from tidewater and don't know as the barnacle *does* stick to the oyster.

Unfortunately, the first object I ever saw in the Sandwich Islands was a repulsive one. It was a case of Oriental leprosy, of so dreadful nature that I have never been able to get it out of my mind since. I don't intend that it shall give a disagreeable complexion to this lecture at all, but inasmuch as it was the first thing I saw in those islands, it naturally suggested itself when I proposed to talk about the islands. It is a very hard matter to get a disagreeable object out of one's memory. I discovered that a good while ago. When I made that funeral excursion in the *Quaker City* they showed me some very interesting objects in a cathedral, and I expected to recollect every one of them—but I didn't. I forgot every one of them—except one—and that I remembered because it was unpleasant. It was a curious piece of ancient sculpture. They don't know where they got it nor how long they have had it. It is a stone figure of a man without any skin—a freshly skinned man showing every vein, artery and tissue. It was the heaviest thing, and yet there was something fascinating about it. It looked so natural; it looked as if it was in pain, and you know a freshly skinned man would naturally look that way. He would unless his attention was occupied with some other matter. It was a dreadful object, and I have been sorry many a time since that I ever saw that man. Sometimes I dream of him, sometimes he is standing by my bedpost, sometimes he is stretched between the sheets, touching me—the most uncomfortable bedfellow I ever had.

I can't get rid of unpleasant recollections. Once when I ran away from school I was afraid to go home at night, so I crawled through a window and laid down on a lounge in my father's office. The moon shed a ghastly light in the room, and presently I decried a long, dark mysterious shape on the floor. I wanted to go and touch it—but I didn't—I restrained myself—I didn't do it. I had a good deal of presence of mind—tried to go to sleep—kept thinking of it. By and by when the moonlight fell upon it, I saw that it was a dead man lying there with his white face turned up in the moonlight. I never was so sick in all my life. I never wanted to take a walk so bad! I went away from there, I didn't hurry—simply went out of the window—and took the sash along with me. I didn't need the sash, but it was handier to take it than to leave it. I wasn't scared, but I was a good deal agitated. I have never forgotten that man. He had fallen dead in the street and they brought him in there to try him, and they brought him in guilty, too.

But I am losing time; what I have been saying don't bear strictly on the Sandwich Islands, but one reminiscence leads to another, and I am obliged to bring myself down in this way, on account of that unpleasant thing that I first saw there. It is not safe to come to any important matter in an entirely direct way. When a young gentleman is about to talk to a young lady about matrimony he don't go straight at it. He begins by talking about the weather. I have done that many a time.

My next remarks will refer to the Sandwich Islands. Now if an impression has gotten abroad in the land that the Sandwich Islands are in South America, that is the error I wish to attack; that is the error I wish to combat. To cut the matter short the Sandwich Isles are 2,000 miles southwest from San Francisco, but why they were put away out there in the middle of the Pacific, so far away from any place and in such an inconvenient locality, is no business of ours—it was the work of providence and is not open to question. The subject is a good deal like many others we should like to inquire into, such as, what mosquitoes were made for, etc., but under the circumstances we naturally feel a delicacy about doing it.

The islands are a dozen in number and their entire area is not greater I suppose than that of Rhode Island and Connecticut combined. They are of volcanic origin, of volcanic construction I should say. There is not a spoonful of legitimate dirt in the whole group, unless it has been imported. Eight of the islands are inhabited, and four of them are entirely girded with a belt of mountains comprising the most productive sugar lands in the world. The sugar lands in Louisiana are considered rich, and yield from 500 to 1,700 pounds per acre. A two-hundred-acre crop of wheat in the States is worth twenty or thirty thousand dollars; a two-hundred-acre crop of sugar in these islands is worth two hundred thousand dollars. You could not do that in this country unless you planted it with stamps and reaped it in bonds. I would go on talking about the sugar interest all night—and I have a notion to do it. But I will spare you. It is very interesting to those who are interested in it, but I'll drop it now. You will find it all in the Patent Office reports, and I can recommend them as the most placid literature in the world.

These islands were discovered some eighty or ninety years ago by Captain Cook, though another man came very near discovering them before, and he was diverted from his course by a manuscript found in a bottle. He wasn't the first man who has been diverted by suggestions got out of a bottle. When these islands were discovered the population was about 400,000, but the white man came and brought various complicated diseases, and education, and civilization, and all sorts of calamities, and consequently the population began to drop off with commendable activity. Forty years ago they were reduced to 200,000, and the educational and civilizing facilities being increased they dwindled down to 55,000, and it is proposed to send a few more missionaries and finish them. It isn't the education or civilization that has settled them; it is the imported diseases, and they have all got the consumption and other reliable distempers, and to speak figuratively they are retiring from business pretty fast. When they pick up and leave we will take possession as lawful heirs.

There are about 3,000 white people in the islands; they are mostly Americans. In fact they are the kings of the Sandwich Islands; the monarchy is not much more than a mere name. These people stand as high in the scale of character as any people in the world, and some of them who were born and educated in those islands don't even know what a vice is. A Kanaka or a native is nobody unless he has a princely income of $75 annually, or a splendid estate worth $100. The country is full of office-holders, and office-seekers; there are plenty of such noble patriots. Of almost any party of three men, two would be office-holders and one an office-seeker. In a little island half the size of one of the wards of St. Louis, there are lots of noblemen, princes and men of high degree, with grand titles, holding big offices, receiving immense salaries—such as ministers of war, secretaries of the navy, secretaries of state and ministers of justice. They make a fine display of uniforms, and are very imposing at a funeral. That's the country for a petty hero to go to, he would soon have the conceit taken out of him. There are so many of them that a nobleman from any other country would be nobody. They only lionize their own people, and therefore they lionize everybody.

In color, the natives are a rich, dark brown—a sort of black and tan. A very pleasing tint. The tropical sun and the easy-going ways inherited from their ancestors, have made them rather idle, but they are not vicious at all, they are good people. The native women in the rural districts wear a loose, magnificent curtain calico garment, but the men don't. Upon great occasions the men wear an umbrella, or some little fancy article like that—further than this they have no inclination toward gorgeousness or attire.

In the old times the king was absolute, his person was sacred, and if even the shadow of a common Kanaka fell upon him the Kanaka had to die. There was no help for him. Whatever the king tabooed it was death to touch or speak of. After the king, came the high priests who sacrificed human victims; after them came the great feudal chiefs, and then the common Kanakas, who were the slaves of all, the wretchedly oppressed. Away down at the bottom of this pyramid were the women, the abject slaves of the whole party. They did all the work and were cruelly mistreated. It was death for a woman to sit at table with her husband, or to eat of the choice fruits of the islands at any time. They seemed to have had a sort of dim knowledge of what came of women eating fruit in the Garden of Eden and they didn't feel justified in taking any more chances. And it is wisdom—unquestionably it is wisdom. Adam wasn't strict enough. Eve broke the *taboo*, and hence comes all this trouble. Can't be too particular about fruit—with women.

They were a rusty set all round—those Kanakas. By and by the American missionaries came and they struck off the shackles from the whole race, breaking the power of the kings and chiefs. They set the common man free, elevated his wife to a position of equality, and gave a spot of land to each to hold forever. The missionaries taught the whole nation to read and write with facility, in the native tongue. I don't suppose there is today a single uneducated person above eight years of age in the Sandwich Islands. It is the best educated country in the world, I believe, not excepting portions of the United States. That has all been done by the American missionaries. And in a large degree it was paid for by the American Sunday school children with their pennies. We all took part in it. True, the system gave opportunities to bad boys. Many a bad boy acquired the habit of confiscating pennies of the missionary cause. But it is one of the proudest recollections of my life that I never did that—at least not more than once or twice. I know that I contributed. I have had nearly $2 invested there for thirty years. But I don't mind it. I don't care for the money if it has been doing good. I don't say this in order to show off, but just mention it as a gentle, humanizing fact that may possibly have a benevolent and beneficent effect upon some members of this audience.

These natives are very hospitable people indeed—very hospitable. If you want to stay a few days and nights in a native's cabin you can stay and welcome. They will do everything they possibly can to make you comfortable.

They will feed you on baked dog, or poi, or raw fish, or raw salt pork, fricasseed cats—all the luxuries of the season. Everything the human heart can desire, they will set before you. Perhaps, now, this isn't a captivating feast at first glance, but it is offered in all sincerity, and with the best motives in the world, and that makes any feast respectable whether it is palatable or not. But if you want to trade, that's quite another matter—that's business! And the Kanucker is ready for you. He is a born trader, and he will swindle you if he can. He will lie straight through, from the first word to the last. Not such lies as you and I tell, but gigantic lies, lies that awe you with their grandeur, lies that stun you with their imperial impossibility. He will sell you a molehill at the market price of a mountain, and will lie it up to an altitude that will make it cheap at the money. If he is caught, he slips out of it with an easy indifference that has an unmistakable charm about it.

One peculiarity of these Kanakas is that nearly every one of them has a dozen mothers—not natural ones—I haven't got down yet where I can make such a statement as that—but adopted mothers. They have a custom of calling any woman mother they take a liking to—no matter what her color or politics—and it is possible for one native to have a thousand mothers if his affections are liberal and stretchy, and most of them are. This custom breeds some curious incidents. A California man went down there and opened a sugar plantation. One of his hands came and said he wanted to bury his mother. He gave him permission. Shortly after he came again with the same request. "I thought you buried her last week," said the gentleman. "This is another one," said the native. "All right," said the gentleman, "go and plant her." Within a month the man wanted by bury some more mothers. "Look here," said the planter, "I don't want to be hard on you in your affliction, but is appears to me that your stock of mothers holds out pretty well. It interferes with business, so clear out, and never come back until you have buried every mother you have in the world."

They are an odd sort of people, too. They can die whenever they want to. That's a fact. They don't mind dying any more than a jilted Frenchman does. When they take a notion to die they die, and it don't make any difference whether there is anything the matter with them or not, and they can't be persuaded out of it. When one of them makes up his mind to die, he just lays down and is just as certain to die as though he had all the doctors in the world hold of him. A gentleman in Hawaii asked his servant if he wouldn't like to die and have a big funeral. He said yes, and looked happy, and the next morning the overseer came and said, "That boy of yours laid down and died last night and said you were going to give him a fine funeral."

They are very fond of funerals. Big funerals are their main weakness. Fine grave clothes, fine funeral appointments, and a long procession are things they take a generous delight in. Years ago a Kanaka and his wife were condemned to be hanged for murder. They received the sentence with manifest satisfaction because it gave an opening for a funeral, you know. It makes but little difference to them whose it is; they would as soon attend their own funeral as anybody else's. This couple were of consequence, and had landed estates. They sold every foot of ground they had and laid it out in fine clothes to be hung in. And the woman appeared on the scaffold in a white satin dress and slippers and feathers of gaudy ribbon, and the man was arrayed in a gorgeous vest, blue clawhammer coat and brass buttons, and white kid gloves. As the noose was adjusted around his neck, he blew his nose with a grand theatrical flourish, so as to show his embroidered white handkerchief. I never, never knew of a couple who enjoyed hanging more than they did.

They are very fond of dogs, these people—not the great Newfoundland or the stately mastiff, but a species of little mean, contemptible cur that a white man would condemn to death on general principles. There is nothing attractive about these dogs—there is not a handsome feature about them, unless it is their bushy tails. A friend of mine said if he had one of these dogs he would cut off the tail and throw the rest of the dog away. They feed this dog, pet him, take ever so much care of him, and then cook and eat him. I couldn't do that. I would rather go hungry for two days than devour an old personal friend in that way; but many a white citizen of those islands throws aside his prejudices and takes his dinner off one of those puppies—and after all it is only our cherished American sausage with the mystery removed.

A Kanaka will eat anything he can bite—a live fish, scales and all, which must be rather annoying to the fish, but the Kanaka doesn't mind that. It used to be said that the Kanakas were cannibals, but that was a slander. They didn't eat Captain Cook—or if they did, it was only for fun. There was one instance of cannibalism. A foreigner, from the South Pacific Islands, set up an office and did eat a good many Kanakas. He was a useful citizen, but had strong political prejudices and used to save up a good appetite for just before election, so that he could thin out the Democratic vote.

At this point in my lecture, in other cities, I usually illustrate cannibalism, but I am a stranger here and don't feel like taking liberties. Still, if any one in the audience will lend me an infant, I will illustrate the matter. But it is of no consequence—it don't matter. I know children have become scarce and high, owing to the inattention they have received since the women's rights movement began. I will leave out that part of my program, though it is very neat and pleasant. Yet it is not necessary, *I* am not hungry.

Well, that foreign cannibal after a while got tired of Kanakas—as most anybody would—and thought he would like to try white man with onions. So he captured and devoured a tough old whaleship captain, but it was the worst thing he ever did. Of course, he could no more digest that old whaler than a keg of nails. There is no telling how much he suffered, with this sin on his conscience and the whaler on his stomach. He lingered for a few days and then died. Now, I don't believe this story myself, and have only told it for its moral. You don't appear to see the moral; but I know there is a moral in it, because I have told it thirty or forty times, and never got a moral out of it yet!

With all these excellent and hospitable ways these Kanakers have some cruel instincts. They will put a live chicken in the fire just it see it hop about. In the olden times they used to be cruel to themselves. They used to tear off their hair and burn their flesh, shave their heads, knock out an eye or a couple of front teeth, when a great person or a king died—just to testify to their sorrow, and if their grief was so sore that they couldn't possibly bear it, they would go out and scalp their neighbor, or burn his house down. It was an excellent custom, too, for it gave every one a good opportunity to square up old grudges. Pity we didn't have it here! They would also kill an infant now and then—bury him alive sometimes; but the missionaries have annihilated infanticide—for my part I can't see why.

The ladies of the Sandwich Islands have a great many pleasant customs which I don't know but we might practice with profit here. The women all ride like men. I wish to introduce that reform in this country. Our ladies ought, by all means to ride like men, these sidesaddles are so dangerous. When women meet each other in the road, they run and kiss and hug each other, and they don't blackguard each other behind each other's backs. I would like to introduce that reform, also. I don't suppose our ladies do it. But they might. But I believe I am getting on dangerous ground. I won't pursue that any further.

These people do nearly everything wrong end first. They buckle the saddle on the right side which is the wrong side; they mount a horse from the wrong side; they turn out on the wrong side to let you go by; they use the same word to say "good-by" and "good morning"; they use "yes" when they mean "no"; the women smoke more than the men do; when they beckon to you to come toward them they always motion in the opposite direction; the only native bird that has handsome feathers has only two, and they are under its wings instead of on top of its head; frequently a native cat has a tail only two inches long and has got a knot tied in the end of it; the native duck lives on the dry tops of mountains 5,000 feet high; the natives always stew chickens instead of baking them; they dance at funerals and sing a dismal heartbroken dirge when they are happy; and with atrocious perverseness they wash your shirts with a club and iron them with a brickbat. In their playing of the noble American game of "seven-up," that's a game, well, I'll explain that by and by. Some of you, perhaps, know all about it, and the rest must guess—but, in their playing of that really noble and intellectual game the dealer deals to his right instead of to his left, and what is insufferably worse—the ten always takes the ace! Now, such abject ignorance as that is reprehensible, and, for one, I am glad the missionaries have gone there.

Now, you see kind of voters you will have if you take those islands away from these people as we are pretty sure to do some day. They will do everything wrong end first. They will make a deal of trouble here too. Instead of fostering and encouraging a judicious system of railway speculation, and all that sort of thing, they will elect the most incorruptible men to Congress. Yes, they will turn everything upside down.

In Honolulu they are the most easy-going people in the world. Some of our people are not acquainted with their customs. They started a gas company once, and put the gas at $13 a thousand feet. They only took in $16 the first month. They all went to bed at dark. They are an excellent people. I speak earnestly. They do not even know the name of some of the vices in this country. A lady called on a doctor. She wanted something for general debility. He ordered her to drink porter. She called him again. The porter had done her no good. He asked her how much porter she had taken. She said a tablespoonful in a tumbler of water. I wish we could import such blessed ignorance into this country. They don't do much drinking there. When they have paid the tax for importing the liquor they have got nothing left to purchase the liquor with. They are very innocent and drink anything that is liquid—kerosene, turpentine, hair oil. In one town, on a Fourth of July, an entire community got drunk on a barrel of Mrs. Winslow's soothing syrup.

The chief glory of the Sandwich Islands is their great volcano. The volcano of Kee-law-ay-oh is 17,000 feet in diameter, and from 700 to 800 feet deep. Vesuvius is nowhere. It is the largest volcano in the world; shoots up flames tremendously high. You witness a serene of unrivaled sublimity, and witness the most astonishing sights. When the volcano of Kee-law-ay-oh broke through a few years ago, lava flowed out of it for twenty days and twenty nights, and made a stream forty miles in length, till it reached the sea, tearing up forests in its awful fiery path, swallowing up huts, destroying all vegetation, rioting through shady dells and sinuous canons. Amidst the carnival of destruction, majestic columns of smoke ascended and formed a cloudy murky pall overhead. Sheets of green, blue, lambent flames were shot upward, and pierced the vast gloom, making all sublimely grand.

The natives are indifferent to volcanic terrors. During the progress of an eruption they ate, drank, bought, sold, planted, builded, apparently indifferent to the roar of consuming forests, the startling detonations, the hissing of escaping steam, the rending of the earth, the shivering and melting of gigantic rocks, the raging and dashing of the fiery waves, the bellowings and unearthly mutterings coming up from a burning deep. They went carelessly on, amid the rain of ashes, sand, and fiery scintillations, gazing vacantly at the ever-varying appearance of the atmosphere, murky, black, livid, blazing, the sudden rising of lofty pillars of flame, the upward curling of ten thousand columns of smoke, and their majestic roll in dense and lurid clouds. All these moving phenomena were regarded by them as the fall of a shower or the running of a brook; while to others they were as the tokens of a burning world, the departing heavens, and a coming judge. There! I'm glad I've got that volcano off my mind.

I once knew a great, tall gawky country editor, near Sacramento, to whom I sent an ode on the sea, starting it with "The long, green swell of the Pacific." The country editor sent back a letter and stated I couldn't fool him, and he didn't want any base insinuations from me. He knew who I meant when I wrote the "long, green swell of the Pacific."

There is one thing characteristic of the tropics that a stranger must have, whether he likes it or not, and that is the boo-hoo fever. Its symptoms are nausea of the stomach, severe headache, backache and bellyache, and a general utter indifference whether school keeps or not. You can't be a full citizen of the Sandwich Islands unless you have the boo-hoo fever. You will never forget it. I remember a little boy who had it once there. A New Yorker asked him if he was afraid to die. He said, "No, I am not afraid to die of anything, except the boo-hoo fever."

The climate of these islands is delightful, it is beautiful. In Honolulu the thermometer stands about 80 or 82 degrees pretty much all the year round—don't change more than 12 degrees in twelve months. In the sugar districts the thermometer stands at 70 and does not change at all. Any kind of thermometer will do—one without any quicksilver is just as good. Eighty degrees by the seashore, and 70 degrees farther inland, and 60 degrees as you ascend the slope of the mountain, and as you go higher 50 degrees, 40, 30, and ever decreasing in temperature, till you get to the top, where it's so cold that you can't speak the truth. I know, for I've been there! The climate is wonderfully healthy, for white people in particular, so healthy that white people venture on the most reckless imprudence. They get up too early; you can see them as early as half-past seven in the morning, and they attend to all their business, and keep it up till sundown. It don't hurt 'em, don't kill 'em, and yet ought to do so. I have seen it so hot in California that greenbacks went up to 142 in the shade.

These Sandwichers believe in a superstition that the biggest liars in the world have got to visit the islands some time before they die. They believe that because it is a fact—you misunderstand—I mean that when liars get there they stay there. They have several specimens they boast of. They treasure up their little perfections, and they allude to them as if the man was inspired—from below. They had a man among them named Morgan. He never allowed anyone to tell a bigger lie than himself, and he always told the last one too. When someone was telling about the natural bridge in Virginia, he said he knew all about it, as his father had helped to build it. Someone was bragging of a wonderful horse he had. Morgan told them of one he had once. While out riding one day a thundershower cane on and chased him for eighteen miles, and never caught him. Not a single drop of rain dropped onto his horse, but his dog was swimming behind the wagon the whole of the way.

Once, when the subject of mean men was being discussed, Morgan told them of an incorporated company of mean men. They hired a poor fellow to blast rock for them. He drilled a hole four feet deep, put in the powder, and began to tamp it down around the fuse. I know all about tamping, as I have worked in a mine myself. The crowbar struck a spark and caused a premature explosion and that man and his crowbar shot up into the air, and he went higher and higher, till he didn't look bigger than a boy, and he kept going higher and higher, until he didn't look bigger than a dog, and he kept on going higher and higher, until he didn't look bigger than a bee, and then he went out of sight; and presently he came in sight again, looking no bigger than a bee, and he came further and further, until he was as big as a dog, and further and further and further, until he was as big as a boy, and he came further and further, until he assumed the full size and shape of a man, and he came down and fell right into the same old spot and went to tamping again. And would you believe it—concluded Morgan—although that poor fellow was not gone more than fifteen minutes, yet that mean company docked him for loss of time.

The land that I have tried to tell you about lies out there in the midst of the watery wilderness, in the very heart of the almost soilless solitudes of the Pacific. It is a dreamy, beautiful, charming land. I wish I could make you comprehend how beautiful it is. It is a land that seems ever so vague and fairy-like when one reads about it in books, peopled with a gentle, indolent, careless race.

It is Sunday land. The land of indolence and dreams, where the air is drowsy and things tend to repose and peace, and to emancipation from the labor, and turmoil, and weariness, and anxiety of life.

"The American Vandal Abroad"

I am to speak of the American Vandal this evening, but I wish to say in advance that I do not use the term in derision, or apply it as a reproach, but I use it because it is convenient and duly and properly modified it best describes the roving, independent, free-and-easy character of that class of traveling Americans who are *not* elaborately educated, cultivated, and refined, and gilded and filigreed with the ineffable graces of the first society. The best class of our countrymen who go abroad keep us well posted about their doings in foreign lands, but their brethren Vandals cannot sing their own praises or publish their adventures.

The American Vandal goes everywhere and is always at home everywhere. He attempts to investigate the secrets of the harems; he views the rock where Paul was let down in a basket, and seriously asks where the basket is. He will choke himself to death trying to make a Turkish pipe and swears it is good. He will go into ecstasies over the insufferable horrors of the Turkish bath, though he is thinking the while that he may never come out alive. He learns to ride a camel. He packs his trunk with figs and other little vegetables. He looks picturesque when beholding Rome from the dome of St. Peter's. His soul is full of admiration. He rises above earthly cares. He is proud and looks proud. His countenance is beaming. He *does not fail to let the public know that he is an American.* This is not a fault. It is commendable. I have seen him in the company of kings and queens, lords and popes. He is always self-possessed, always untouched, unabashed—even in the presence of the Sphinx.

The American Vandal gallops over England, Scotland, Spain and Switzerland, and finally brings up in Italy. He thinks it is the proper thing to visit Genoa, the stately old City of Palaces, whose vast marble edifices almost meet together over streets so narrow that three men can hardly walk abreast in them and so crooked that a man generally comes out of them about the same place he went in at. He only stays in Genoa long enough to see a few celebrated things and get some fragments of stone from the house Columbus was born in—for your genuine Vandal is an intolerable and incorrigible relic-gatherer. It is estimated that if all the fragments of stone brought from Columbus's house by travelers were collected together they would suffice to build a house 14,000 feet long and 16,000 feet high and I suppose they would.

Next he hurries to Milan and takes notes of the Grand Cathedral: (for he is always taking notes). Oh, I remember Milan and the noble Cathedral well enough—that marble miracle of enchanting architecture. I remember how we entered and walked about its vast spaces and among its huge columns, gazing aloft at the monster windows all aglow with brilliantly colored scenes in the life of the Savior and his followers. And I remember the sideshows and curiosities there, too. The guide showed us a coffee-colored piece of sculpture which he said was considered to have come from the hand of Phidias, since it was not possible that any other man, of any epoch, could have copied nature with such faultless accuracy. The figure was that of a man without a skin; with every vein, artery, muscle, every fibre and tendon and tissue of the human frame, represented in minute detail. It looked natural because it looked somehow *as if it were in pain.* A skinned man *would be likely to look that way*—unless his attention were occupied by some other matter. It was a hideous thing, and yet there was a fascination about it somewhere. I am very sorry I saw it, because I shall *always* see it now. I shall dream of it, sometime, I shall dream that it is resting its corded arms on the bed's head and looking down on me with its dead eyes; I shall dream that it is stretched between the sheets with me and touching me with its exposed muscles and its stringy cold legs.

They have many holy relics in the Cathedral of Milan. The priest showed us two of St. Paul's fingers and one of St. Peter's; and a bone of Judas Iscariot—it was a black one—and bones and little vessels of blood of St. John, St. Mark, and several other of the disciples. They keep these relics in vials, in a glass case, and have them labeled as we often see geological specimens. And they showed us a handkerchief in which the Savior had left the impression of his face (we saw another in Rome afterward), and a piece of the stone the angels rolled away from the door of the Holy Sepulchre (we saw the whole of the stone afterward in Jerusalem)—and a part of the real crown of thorns (we saw a whole one at Notre Dame in Paris)—and a fragment of the purple robe worn by the Savior, a nail from the True Cross and a picture of the Virgin and Child painted by the veritable hand of St. Luke. In every cathedral into which the American Vandal wanders, all over Europe, and especially Italy, he finds repetitions of these same relics—until finally he becomes so accustomed to them, and so attached to them that a cathedral that hasn't a pretended splinter of the Cross, or piece of a saint or fragment of a martyr to show, has no charm for *him*. I knew one of these gentry—a simple-minded, innocent Vandal, he was and very vulgar—who had a perfect *passion* for these things. Whenever he went into a great cathedral—when everybody was going into ecstasies over the grand architecture and paintings and such things, he'd beckon to a priest and say, "Here, friend, stuffy, trot out your relics!" He didn't mean any disrespect but that was his way, you know.

The Vandal goes to see the ancient and most celebrated painting in the world, "The Last Supper"—we all know it in engravings: the disciples all sitting on [one] side of a long plain table, and Christ with bowed head in the center—all the last suppers in the world are copied from this painting. It is so damaged now, by the wear and tear of three hundred years that the figures can hardly be distinguished. The Vandal goes to see this picture, which all the world praises—looks at it with a critical eye and says it's a perfect old nightmare of a picture and he wouldn't give forty dollars for a million like it—(and I share his opinion), and then he is done with Milan.

He paddles around the Lake of Como for a few days, and then takes the cars. He is bound for Venice, the oldest and the proudest and the princeliest Republic that ever graced the earth. We put on a good many airs with our little infant Republic of a century's growth, but we grow modest when we stand before this gray, old, imperial city that was a haughty, invincible, magnificent Republic for fourteen hundred years! The Vandal is bound for Venice! He has a long, weary ride of it, but just as the day is closing he hears someone shout, "*Venice!*" and puts his head out of the window, and sure enough, afloat on the placid sea, a league away, lies the great city with its towers and domes and steeples drowsing in a golden mist of sunset!

Have you been to Venice-and seen the winding canals, and the stately edifices that border them all along, ornamented with the quaint devices and sculptures of a former age?—and have you seen the great Cathedral of St. Mark's—and the Giant's Staircase—and the famous Bridge of Sighs—and the great Square of St. Mark's—and the ancient pillar, with the winged lion of St. Mark that stands on it, whose story and whose origin are a mystery—and the Rialto, where Shylock used to loan money on human flesh and other collateral?—And have you seen the gondolas and heard the romantic gondolier sing—as only the romantic gondolier *can* sing—according to the romances? *I* have heard the romantic gondoliers sing—we had just entered Venice at eight in the evening and were floating away toward the hotel. We were poking dismally around in the shadows among long rows of towering untenanted buildings, and were very sad and disheartened and disappointed—for *this* was not the Venice we had expected. It was at such a time as this that this ragged, barefooted guttersnipe turned up and began to sing, true to the traditions of his race.

I stood it for about five minutes—and then I said: "Look here, Roderigo Gonzales Michael Angelo—Smith—I'm a pilgrim and I'm a stranger, but I'm not going to stand any such caterwauling as that! If this thing goes on one of us has [to] take water. It is enough that my cherished dreams of Venice have been blighted forever, without taxing *your* talents to make the matter worse. Another yelp out of you and overboard you go!"

I had begun to feel that the old Venice of song and story had departed forever. But I was too hasty. In a few minutes we swept gracefully out into the Grand Canal, and under the mellow moonlight the Venice of poetry and romance stood revealed. Right from the water's edge rose stately palaces of marble; gondolas were gliding swiftly hither and thither and disappearing suddenly through unsuspected gates and alleys; ponderous stone bridges threw their shadows athwart the glittering waves. There was life and motion everywhere, and yet everywhere there was a hush, a stealthy sort of stillness, that was suggestive of secret enterprises of bravos and of lovers; and clad half in moonbeams and half in mysterious shadows, the grim old mansions of the Republic seemed to have an expression about them of having an eye out for just such enterprises as these at that moment. Music came stealing over the waters—Venice was complete.

The gondola is an institution. But it seems queer—ever so queer—this thing of a boat doing duty as a private carriage. In Venice we see business men come to the front door, portly fellows, with their portliness gauged according to their incomes, step into a *gondola*, instead of a street car, and go off down town to the counting-house. We see young ladies, out visiting, stand on the stoop, and laugh, chatter, and flirt their fans, and kiss good-by, and say "Come *soon*. Maria, no *do*—you've been just as mean as ever you *could*—and mother's dying to see you, and so's the poodle and the cat and everybody—and Oh, we've moved into the new house, and Oh it's such a *love* of a place—so convenient to the post office, and the church, and the Y.M.C.A.—and we do have such fishing and such carrying on and *such* swimming matches in the back yard—Oh you *must* come—no distance at all—and if you go down through by St. Mark's and the Bridge of Sighs and out through the alley and come up by Santa Maria del Frari, and into the Grand Canal, there isn't a *bit* of current—now *do* come, Sally Maria—by-bye!" and then the little humbug trips down the steps, jumps into the gondola—says under her breath, "Disagreeable old thing I hope she *won't* come!"—goes skimming away around the corner, and the other girl slams the street door and says, "Well, that infliction's over, anyway—but I suppose I've *got* to go and see her—tiresome, stuck-up thing!"

Ah, human nature is just the same, all over the world—and *girls* are just the same everywhere—the girls in Venice are just like the girls in

Cleveland—*they* wear their dresses cut bias—certainly—and put the most gorgeous gussets on 'em, and gores and all that sort of thing—and wad up their hair behind so bewitchingly and prop it up with a crupper—and *they* keep a pet kangaroo so as they can see how to do the Grecian Bend right. Ah the girls in Venice are precisely like the girls in Pittsburgh—a Venice girl is as *much like* a Pittsburgh girl as—as—as one *blessed* angel is like another! (That was a close place—but I rubbed through.)

And we see the diffident young man, *mild* of moustache, *affluent* of hair, *indigent* of brain, *elegant* of costume, drive up in his gondola to *her* father's mansion—tell his hackman to—*bail out* and wait—start fearfully up the steps and meet the *old man* right on the threshold!—hear him ask what street the new British bank is in—as if *that* were what he came for—and then bounce into his boat and scurry away with his coward heart in his boots!—see him come sneaking around the corner again directly, with a corner of the gondola curtain open toward the old gentleman's disappearing gondola—and then out scampers his Susan with a flock of little Italian endearments fluttering from her lips and goes to drive with him in the watery avenues away down toward the Rialto.

We see the ladies go out shopping, in the most natural way, and flit from street to street, and from store to store, just in the good old fashion, except that they leave the gondola instead of a private carriage waiting for them a couple of hours at the curbstone—waiting while they make the nice young clerks pull down tons and tons of silks and velvets and bombazine and bobbinett and moire antiques and solferino and all those splendid fabrics—and then they buy a paper of pins and go paddling up the canal to confer a portion of their disastrous patronage on the other stores. And they always have their purchases *sent home* just in the good old way. Ah, human nature is *very* much the same all over the world—and it was *so* like my dear native home to see a lady buy ten cents' worth of blue ribbon and—have it sent home in a scow. Ah, these little touches of nature move one almost to tears in those far-off foreign lands! Human nature is just the same all over the world. Blessed Woman—her ways of pleasantness and all her paths are peace.

I love the whole sex—my own mother was a woman.

And we see little girls and boys go out for an airing, with their nurses, in the gondola—when they've been good and haven't stolen any jam, nor told any lies they couldn't substantiate. *I* never had any trouble about going out for an airing, when *I* was young—because I never stole jam—when I could get my little brother to steal it for me—and I always made it a point to be just as particular about telling a lie as if I were telling the truth. I'd rather have a sound judgement than *talent*.

And we see staid families, with prayer book and beads, enter the gondola, dressed in their Sunday best, and float solemnly away to church.

At midnight we see the theater break up and discharge its swarm of chattering youth and beauty, hear the cries of the hackman-gondoliers and behold the struggling crowd jump aboard the black multitude of boats and go skimming down the moonlit avenues—we see them branching off, here and there and disappearing up divergent streets; we hear the faint sounds of laughter, of shouted farewells floating up out of the distance—and then, the strange pageant being gone, we have lonely stretches of glittering water, of stately buildings, of blotting shadows, of weird stone faces creeping into the moonlight, of deserted bridges, of motionless boats at anchor—and over all broods that mysterious stillness, that stealthy quiet, that befits so well this old dreaming Venice!

Our Vandals hurried away from Venice and scattered abroad everywhere. You could find them breaking specimens from the dilapidated tomb of Romeo and Juliet at Padua—and infesting the picture galleries of Florence—and risking their necks on the Leaning Tower of Pisa—and snuffing sulphur fumes on the summit of Vesuvius—and burrowing among the exhumed wonders of Herculaneum and Pompeii—and you might see them with spectacles on and blue cotton umbrellas under their arms benignantly contemplating Rome from the venerable arches of the Coliseum.

And finally we sailed from Naples, and in due time anchored before the Piraeus, the seaport of Athens in Greece. But the quarantine was in force, and so they set a guard of soldiers to watch us and would not let us go ashore, However, I and three other Vandals took a boat, and muffled the oars, and slipped ashore at 11:30 at night, and dodged the guard successfully. Then we made a wide circuit around the slumbering town, avoiding all roads and houses—for they'd about as soon hang a body as not for violating the quarantine laws in those countries. We got around the town without any accident, and then struck out across the Attic Plain, steering straight for Athens—over rocks and hills, and brambles and everything—with Mt. Helicon for a landmark. And so we tramped five or six miles. The Attic Plain is a mighty uncomfortable plain to travel in, even if it is *so* historical. The armed guards got after us three times and flourished their gleaming gun barrels in the moonlight, because they thought we were stealing grapes occasionally—and the fact is we *were*—for we found by and by that the brambles that tripped us up so often were grape vines—but these people in the country didn't know that we were quarantine blockade-runners, and so they only scared us and jawed Greek at us, and let us go, instead of arresting us.

We didn't care about Athens particularly, but we wanted to see the famous Acropolis and its ruined temples, and we did. We climbed the steep hill of the Acropolis about one in the morning and tried to storm that grand old fortress that had scorned the battles and sieges of three thousand years. We had the garrison out, mighty quick—four Greeks—and we bribed them to betray the citadel and unlock the gates. In a moment we stood in the presence of the noblest ruins we had ever seen—the most elegant, the most graceful, the most imposing. The renowned Parthenon towered above us, and about us were the wreck of what were once the snowy marble Temples of Hercules and a second Minerva, and another whose name I have forgotten. Most of the Parthenon's grand columns are still standing, but the roof is gone.

As we wandered down the marble paved length of this mighty temple, the scene was strangely impressive. Here and there in lavish profusion were gleaming white statues of men and women, propped against blocks of marble, some of them armless, some without legs, others headless—but all looking mournful and sentient, and startlingly human! They rose up and confronted the midnight intruder on every side—they stared at him with stony eyes from unlooked-for nooks and recesses; they peered at him over fragmentary heaps for down the desolate corridors; they barred his way in the midst of the broad forum, and solemnly pointed with handless arms the way from the sacred fane; and through the roofless temple the moon looked down and banded the floor and darkened the scattered fragments and broken statues with the slanting shadows of the columns!

What a world of ruined sculpture was about us! Stood up in rows—stacked up in piles—scattered broadcast over the wide area of the Acropolis—were hundreds of crippled statues of all sizes and of the most exquisite workmanship; and vast fragments of marble that once belonged to the entablatures, covered with bas-reliefs representing battles and sieges, ships of war with three and four tiers of oars, pageants and processions—everything one could think of.

We walked out into the grass-grown, fragment-strewn court beyond the Parthenon. It startled us, every now and then, to see a stony white face stare suddenly up at us out of the grass with its dead eyes. The place seemed alive with ghosts. We half expected to see the Athenian heroes of twenty centuries ago glide out of the shadows and steal into the old temple they knew so well and regarded with such boundless pride.

The full moon was riding high in the cloudless heavens, now. We sauntered carelessly and unthinkingly to the edge of the lofty battlements of the citadel, and looked down—and lo, a vision! And *such* a vision! Athens by moonlight! All the beauty in all the world combined could not rival it! The prophet that thought the splendors of the New Jerusalem were revealed to him, surely saw this instead. It lay in the level plain right under our feet—all spread abroad like a picture—and we looked down upon it as we might have looked from a balloon. We saw no semblance of a street, but every house, every window, every clinging vine, every projection, was as distinct and sharply marked as if the time were noonday; and yet there was no glare, no glitter, nothing harsh or repulsive—the silent city was flooded with the mellowest light that ever streamed from the moon, and seemed like some living creature wrapped in peaceful slumber. On its further side was a little temple whose delicate pillars and ornate front glowed with a rich lustre that chained the eye like a spell; and nearer by the palace of the King reared its creamy walls out of the midst of a great garden of shrubbery that was flecked all over with a random shower of amber lights—a spray of golden sparks that lost their brightness in the glory of the moon and glinted softly upon the sea of dark foliage like the pallid stare of the milky way! Overhead the stately columns, majestic still in their ruin—under foot the dreaming city—in the distance the silver sea—not on the broad earth is there another picture half so beautiful!

We got back to the ship safely, just as the day was dawning. We had walked upon pavements that had been pressed by Plato, Aristotle, Demosthenes, Socrates, Phocion, Euclid, Xenophon, Herodotus, Diogenes, and a hundred others of deathless fame, and were satisfied. We got to stealing grapes again on the way back, and half a dozen rascally guards with muskets and pistols captured us and marched us in the center of a hollow square nearly to the sea—till we were well beyond all the graperies. Military escort—ah, I never traveled in so much state in all my life.

I leave Vandal here. I have not time to follow *him* further—nor *our* Vandals to Constantinople and Smyrna and the Holy Land, Egypt, the Islands of the Sea and to Russia and his visit to the Emperor. But I wish I *could* tell of that visit of our gang of *Quaker City* Vandals to the grandest monarch of the age, America's stanch, old, steadfast Friend, Alexander II, Autocrat of Russia!

The Emperor is a man of noble presence—tall and spare—has a kind blue eye—looks great and *good* and every inch an Emperor. It was a novel sensation to stand in the presence of this man, chatting easily and pleasantly like an ordinary mortal, and so simply dressed—yet whose slightest word is law to 70,000,000 of human beings!—who could open his lips and ships would fly through the waves, locomotives would speed over the plains, couriers would hurry from village to village, a hundred telegraphs would flash the word to the four corners of an Empire that stretches its vast proportions over a seventh part of the habitable globe, and a countless multitude of men would spring to do his bidding! If this man sprained his ankle, a million miles of telegraph would carry the news over mountains—valleys—under the trackless sea—and ten thousand newspapers would prate of it; if he were grievously ill, all the nations would know it before the sun rose again—if he dropped lifeless where he stood, the effect might be felt in the furthest lands of Christendom! Yet where I stood, worm of the dust as I am, I could have overturned this god—I could have knocked this colossus down with *my* feeble fist—but I restrained myself.

If there is a moral to this lecture it is an injunction to all Vandals to *travel*; I am glad the American Vandal *goes* abroad. It does him good. It makes a better *man* of him. It rubs out a multitude of his old unworthy biases and prejudices. It aids his religion for it enlarges his charity and his benevolence and it broadens his views of men and things; it deepens his generosity and his compassion for the failings and short-comings of his fellow creatures. Contact with men of various nations and many creeds, teaches him that there are *other* people in the world besides his own little clique, and other opinions as worthy of attention and respect as his own. He finds that he and *his* are not the most momentous matters in the universe. Cast into trouble and misfortune in strange lands and being mercifully cared for by those he never saw before, he begins to learn the best lesson of all—that one which culminates in the conviction that God puts *something* good and something loveable in every man His hands create—that the world is *not* a cold, harsh, cruel prison-house, stocked with all manner of selfishness and hate and wickedness. It *liberalizes* the Vandal to travel—you never saw a bigoted, opinionated, stubborn, narrow-minded, self-conceited, *almighty mean man* in your life but he had stuck in one place since he was born and thought God made the world and dyspepsia and bile for *his* especial comfort and satisfaction. So I say *by all means*, let the American Vandal *go on* traveling, and let no man discourage him. Remember.

Our Vandals in the *Quaker City* will never regret their pilgrimage—they learned something—matters that were useful—other matters that were only pleasant. Much that they learned, much that they saw, much that they heard, they will forget—but still a store of softly-tinted images will remain in their memories—and float through their reveries and dreams for many and many a year to come. They will remember *some*thing.

"Roughing It Lecture"

Ladies and gentlemen: By request of the chairman of the committee, who has been very busy, and is very tired, I suppose, I ask leave to introduce to you the lecturer of the evening, Mr. Clemens, otherwise Mark Twain, a gentleman whose great learning, whose historical accuracy, whose devotion to science, and whose veneration for the truth, are only equaled by his high moral character and his majestic presence. I refer in these vague and general terms to myself. I am a little opposed to the custom of ceremoniously introducing a lecturer to an audience, partly because it seems to me that it is not entirely necessary where a man has been pretty well advertised, and partly because it makes a lecturer feel uncomfortably awkward. But where it is necessary I would much rather make it myself. Then I can get in all the facts.

But it is not really the introduction that I care for—I don't care about that—that don't discommode me—but it's the compliments that sometimes go with it. That's what *hurts*. It would hurt anybody. The idea of a young lady being introduced into society as the sweetest singer or the finest conversationalist! You might as well knock her in the head at once. She could not say a word the rest of the evening. I never had but one public introduction that seemed to me just exactly the thing—an introduction brimful of grace. Why, it was a sort of inspiration. And yet the man who made it wasn't acquainted with me; but he was sensible to the backbone, and he said to me: "Now, you don't want any compliments?" I said he was exactly right, I *didn't* want any compliments. And when he introduced me he said, "Ladies and gentlemen, I shan't fool away any unnecessary time in this introduction. I don't know anything about this man; at least I know only two things; one is, that he has never been in the penitentiary; and the other is, I don't know why." Such an introduction as that puts a man at his ease right off.

Now when I first started out on this missionary expedition, I had a lecture which I liked very well, but by and by I got tired of telling that same old stuff over and over again, and then I got up another lecture, and after that another one, and I am tired of that; so I just thought tonight I would try something fresh, if you are willing. I don't suppose you care what a lecturer talks about if he only tells the truth—at intervals. Now I have got a book in press (it will be out pretty soon), over 600 octavo pages, and illustrated after the fashion of the *Innocents Abroad.* Terms—however I am not around canvassing for the work. I should like to talk a little of that book to you tonight. It is very fresh in my mind, as it is not more than three months since I wrote it. Say thirty or forty pages—or if you prefer it the whole 600.

Ten or twelve years ago, I crossed the continent from Missouri to California, in the old overland stagecoach, a good while before the Pacific Railway was built. Over 1,900 miles. It was a long ride, day and night, through sagebrush, over sand and alkali plains, wolves and Indians, starvation and smallpox—everything to make the journey interesting. Had a splendid time, a most enjoyable pleasure trip, in that old stagecoach. We were bound for Nevada, which was then a brand-new Territory nearly or about as large as the state of Ohio. It was a desolate, barren, sterile, mountainous, unpeopled country, sagebrush and deserts of alkali. You could scarcely cast your eye in any direction but your gaze would be met by one significant object, and that was the projecting horns of a dried shrunken carcass of an ox, preaching eloquent sermons of the hardships suffered by those emigrants, where a soil refused to clothe its nakedness, except now and then a little rill (or, as you might call it, a river) goes winding through the plain. Such is the Carson River, which clothes the valley with refreshing and fragrant hay fields. However, hay is a scant crop, and with all the importations from California the price of that article has never come under $300 a ton. In the winter the price reaches $800, and once went up to $1,200 per ton, and then the cattle were turned out to die, and it is hardly putting the figures too strong to say that the valleys were paved with the remains of these cattle.

It is a land where the winters are long and rigorous, where the summers are hot and scorching, and where not a single drop of rain ever falls during eleven tedious months; where it never thunders, and never lightens; where no river finds its way to the sea, or empties its waters into the great lakes that have no perceptible outlet, and whose surplus waters are spirited through mysterious channels down into the ground. A territory broad and ample, but which has not yet had a population numbering 80,000, yet a country that produced $20,000,000 of silver bullion in the year 1863, and produces $12,000,000 to $16,000,000 every year, yet the population has fallen away until now it does not number more than 15,000 or 18,000. Yet that little handful of people vote just as strongly as they do anywhere, are just as well represented in the Senate of the United States as Michigan, or the great state of New York with her 3,000,000 or 4,000,000 of people. That is equality in representation.

I spoke of sagebrush. That is a particular feature of the country out there. It's an interesting sort of shrub. You see no other sort of vegetable, and clear from Pike's Peak to California's edge, the sagebrushes stand from three to six feet apart, one vast greenish-gray sea of sagebrush. It was the emigrant's fast friend, his only resource for fuel. In its appearance it resembles a venerable live oak with its rough bark and knotty trunk, everything twisted and dwarfed, covered with its thick foliage. I think the sagebrush are beautiful—one at a time is, anyway. Of course, when you see them as far as the eye can reach, seven days and a half in the week, it is different. I am not trying to get up an excitement over sagebrush, but there are many reasons why it should have some mention from an appreciative friend.

I grant you that as a vegetable for table use sagebrush is a failure. Its leaves taste like our ordinary sage; you can make sage tea of it, but anybody in this audience who has ever been a boy, or a girl, or both, in a country where doctors were scarce and measles and grandmothers plenty, don't hanker after sage tea. And yet after all there was a manifest Providence in the creation of sagebrush, for it is food for the mules and donkeys, and therefore many emigrant trains are enabled to pull through with their loads where ox teams would lie down and die of starvation. That a mule will eat anything. He don't give the toss-up of a copper between oysters, lead pipe, brick dust, or even patent office reports. He takes whatever he can get most of.

In our journey we kept climbing and climbing for I don't know many days and nights. At last we reached the highest eminence—the extreme summit of the great range of the Rocky Mountains, and entered the celebrated South Pass. Now the South Pass is more suggestive of a straight road than a suspension bridge hung in the clouds, though in one place it suggests the latter. One could look below him on the diminishing crags and canons lying down, down, down, away to the vague plain below, with a crooked thread in it which was the road, and tufts of feathers in it which were trees—the whole country spread out like a picture, sleeping in the sunlight, and darkness stealing over it, blotting out feature after feature under the frown on a gathering storm—not a film or shadow to mar the spectator's gaze. I could watch the storm break forth down there; could see the lightnings flash, the sheeted rain drifting along the canon's side, and hear the thunder crash upon crash, reverberating among a thousand rocky cliffs. This is a familiar experience to traveling people. It was a miracle of sublimity to a boy like me, who could hardly say that he had ever been away from home a single day in his life before.

We visited Salt Lake City in our journey. Carson City, the capital of

Nevada, had a wild harum-scarum population of editors, thieves, lawyers, in fact all kinds of blacklegs. Its desperadoes, gamblers, and silver miners were armed to the teeth, every one of them dressed in the roughest kind of costumes, which looked strange and romantic to me and I was fascinated.

Everybody rode horseback in that town. I never saw such magnificent horsemanship as that displayed in Carson streets every day, and I did envy them, though I was not much of a horseman. But I had soon learned to tell a horse from a cow, and was burning with impatience to learn more. I was determined to have a horse and ride myself. Whilst this thought was rankling in my mind, the auctioneer came scouring through the plaza on a black beast, that was humped like a dromedary, and fearfully homely. He was going at "twenty, twenty-two-two dollars, for horse, saddle, and bridle."

A man standing near me—whom I didn't know—but who turned out to be the auctioneer's brother, noticed the wistful look in my eye, and observed that was a remarkable horse to be going at such a price, let alone the saddle and bridle. I said I had half a notion to bid. "Now," he says, "I know that horse. I know him well. You are a stranger, I take it. You might think he is an American horse, but he is not anything of the kind. He is a Mexican plug—that's what he is—a genuine Mexican plug," but there was something else about that man's way of saying it, that made me just determined that I would own a genuine Mexican plug—if it took every cent I had. And I said, "Has he any other advantages?" He hooked his forefinger in the pocket of my army shirt, and led me to one side, and in a low tone so that no one else could hear said, "Sh! don't say a word! He can outbuck any horse in America; he can outbuck any horse in the world." Just then the auctioneer came along. "Twenty-four, twenty-four dollars, for the horse, saddle and bridle." I said, "Twenty-seven!" "Sold!"

I took the genuine Mexican plug, paid for him, put him in a livery stable, let him get something to eat, and get rested, and then in the afternoon I brought him out in the plaza, and some of the citizens held him by the head, and others held him down to the earth by the tail, and I got on him. As soon as those people let go he put all his feet in a bunch together, let his back sag down, and then he arched it up suddenly, and shot me one hundred and eighty yards; and I came down again, straight down, and lighted in the saddle, and went up again. And when I came down the next time I lit on his neck, and seized him, and slid back into the saddle, and held on. Then he raised himself straight up in the air and on his hind feet, and just walked around awhile, like a member of Congress, and then he came down and went up the other way, and just walked around on his hands, just as a schoolboy would. Then he came down on all fours again with the same old process of shooting me up in the air, and the third time I went up I heard a man say, "Oh, don't he buck!" So that was "bucking." I was very glad to know it. Not that I was enjoying it, but then I had been taking a general sort of interest in it, and had naturally desired to know what the name of it was. And whilst I was up somebody hit the horse a whack with a strap, and when I came down again the genuine bucker was gone.

While this performance was going on, a sympathizing crowd had gathered around, and one of them remarked to me, "Stranger, you have been taken in. That's a genuine Mexican plug," and another one says, "Think of it! You might have bought an American horse, used to all kinds of work, for a very little more money." Well I didn't want to talk. I didn't have anything to say. I was so jolted up, so internally, externally and eternally mixed up, gone all to pieces. I put my hand on my forehead, and the other on my stomach; and if I had been the owner of sixteen hands I could have found a place for every one of them.

Now if you would see the noblest, loveliest inland lake in the world, you should go to Lake Tahoe. It is just on the boundary line between California and Nevada. I have seen some of the world's celebrated lakes and they bear no comparison with Tahoe. There it is, a sheet of perfectly pure, limpid water, lifted up 6,300 feet above the sea—a vast oval mirror framed in a wall of snow-clad mountain peaks, above the common world. Solitude is king, and in that realm calm silence is brooding always. It is the home of rest and tranquility and gives emancipation and relief from the griefs and plodding cares of life.

Could you but see the morning breaking there, gilding those snowy summits and then creeping gradually along the slopes until it sets the lake and woodlands free from mist, all agleam, you would see old Nature, the master artist, painting those dissolving views on the still water and finally grouping all these features into a complete picture. Every little dell, the mountains with their dome-turned pinnacles, the cataracts and drifting clouds, are all exquisitely photographed on the burnished surface of the lake, suffused with the softest and richest color.

This lake is ten miles from Carson City, and in company with a friend we used to foot it out there, taking along provisions and blankets—camp out on the lake shore two or three weeks at a time; not another human being within miles of us. We used to loaf about in the boat, smoke and read, sometimes play seven-up to strengthen the mind. It's a sinful game, but it's mighty nice. We'd just let the boat drift and drift wherever it wanted to. I can stand a deal of such hardship and suffering when I'm healthy. And the water was so wonderfully clear. Where it was eight feet deep the pebbles on the bottom were just as distinct as if you held them in your hand; and in that clear white atmosphere it seemed as if the boat was drifting through the air. Out in the middle it was a deep dark indigo blue, and the official measurement made by the State Geologist of California shows it to be 1,525 feet deep in the center. You can imagine that it would take a great many churches and steeples piled one upon another before they would be perceptible above its surface. You might use up a great deal of ecclesiastical architecture in that way. Now, notwithstanding that lake is lifted so high among the clouds, surrounded by the everlasting snow-capped mountain peaks, with its surface higher than Mt. Washington in the East, and notwithstanding the water is pretty shallow around the edges, yet the coldest winter day in the recollection of humanity was never known to form ice upon its surface. It has no feeders but the little mountain rills, yet it never rises nor falls. Donner Lake, close by, freezes hard every winter. Why Lake Tahoe does not, is a question which no scientist has ever been able to explain.

If there are any consumptives here I urge them to go out there, renew their age, make their bodies hale and hearty, in the pure magnificent air of Lake Tahoe. If it don't cure them, I will bury them—I shall be glad to do it. I will give them a funeral that will be a comfort to them as long as they live. But it *will* cure them. I met a man there—he had been a man once—now he was nothing but a shadow and a very poor shadow at that—and that man had come there deliberately to die, and what a sickly failure he made of it! He was in dead earnest. He had heard that this air was easy and soothing to breathe, as God knows it is; and he had simply come out there to have what comfort he might whilst life ebbed away. And he had brought along a plan of his private graveyard, and pictures and drawings of different kinds of coffins and hearses, and such things; and he never did anything but sit around and study that graveyard, and figure at coffins, and such things, trying to make up his mind which kind he liked best, or which kind would be most becoming.

Well, I met that man three months afterward. He was chasing mountain sheep over mountains seven miles high, with a Sharps' rifle. He didn't get them, but he was chasing them just the same. He had used up his graveyard plans and things for wadding and had sent home for some more. Such a cure as that was! Why, when I first saw that man his clothes fitted him about as a circus tent fits the tent-pole; now they were snug to him; they stuck to him like postage stamps, and he weighed a ton. Yes, he weighed more than a ton, but I will throw in the odd ounces. I'm not particular about that, eleven I think it was. I know what I am talking about, for I took him to a hay scales and weighed him myself. A lot of us stood on there with him. But really, that was a remarkable cure. I have exaggerated it a little. You might not have noticed it. But still it was a cure and a very remarkable one. I wish you would not heed my nonsense, but simply take note of my earnest word. I think if I could only persuade one invalid to go out there I should feel as if I had done one thing worth having accomplished, I am really sincere about that.

And if there is a sportsman in this audience, I say to him, shoulder your gun and go out there. It's the noblest hunting ground on earth. You can hunt there a year and never find anything—except mountain sheep; but you can't get near enough to shoot one. You can see plenty of them with a spyglass. It is our American Shamwah (I believe that is the way the word is pronounced—I don't know), with enormous horns, inhabiting the roughest mountain fastnesses, so exceedingly wild that it is impossible to get within rifle-shot of it. There was no other game in that country when I was there—except seven-up; though one can see a California quail now and then—a proud, stately, beautiful bird, with a curved and graceful plum on top of its head. But you can't shoot one. You might as well try to kill a cast iron dog. They don't mind a mortal wound any more than a man would mind a scratch.

I had supposed in my innocence that silver mining was nice, easy business, and that of course silver lay around loose on the hillsides, and that all you had to do was to pick it up, and that you could tell it from any other substance on account of its brightness and its white metallic look. Then came my disappointment; for I found that silver was merely scattered through quartz rock. Gold is found in cement veins, in quartz veins, loosely mingled with the earth, in the sand in beds of rivers, but I never heard of any other house or home for silver to live in than quartz rock. This rock is of a dull whitish color faintly marked with blue veins. A fine powder of silver ore makes these blue veins and this yields $30 in bullion. A little dab of silver that I could crowd in my mouth came out of this 2,000 pounds of solid rock. I found out afterward that thirty-dollar rock was mighty profitable. Then they showed me some more rock which was a little more clouded, that was worth $50 a ton. The bluer and darker the rock the richer it was. Sometimes you could find it worth $400, $500 and $600 a ton. At rare intervals rock can be found that is worth $1,500 and $2,000 per ton, and at rarer intervals you would see a piece of quartz that had a mass of pure silver in its grip, large as a child's head—more than pure, because it always has a good deal of gold mixed up in its composition. The wire silver is Nature's aristocratic jewelry. The quartz crystallizes and becomes perfectly clear, just as clear and faultless as the diamond, and almost as radiant in beauty. Nature, down there in the depths of the earth, takes one of these quartz rocks, shapes a cavity, and right in its heart imprisons a delicate little coil of serpentine, pure white, aristocratic silver.

It was uphill work, this silver mining. There were plenty of mines, but it required a fortune to work one; for tons of worthless rock must be ground to powder to get at the silver. I was the owner of a hundred silver mines, yet I realized that I was the poorest man on earth. Couldn't sell to anybody; couldn't pay my board; so I had to go to work in a quartz mill at ten dollars a week. A nice place, truly, for the proprietor of a hundred silver mines! I was glad to get that berth, but I couldn't keep it. I don't know why; I was the most careful workman they ever had. They said so. I took more pains with my work than anybody else. I was shoveling sand—tailings as they call it. It is silver-bearing rock that has been ground up and worked over once. It is then saved and worked over again. I was so particular about it that I have sat still for one hour and a half and studied about the best way to shovel that sand. And if I couldn't cipher it out in my mind just so, I wouldn't go shoveling around recklessly—I would leave it alone until the next day. Many a time when I have been carrying sand from one pile to another, thirty or forty feet apart. I would get started with a pailful when a splendid idea would strike me and I would carry that sand right back and sit down and think about it. Like as not I would get so absorbed in it as to go to sleep. I almost always go to sleep when I am excited.

Why, I always knew there must be some tiptop, first-rate way to move that sand. At last I discovered it. I went to the boss, and told him that I had got just the thing, the very best and quickest way to get that sand from one pile to the other. And he says, "I'm awful glad to hear it." You never saw a man so uplifted as he was. It appeared to take a load off his breast—a load of sand, I suppose. And I said, "What you want now is a cast iron pipe about thirteen or fourteen feet in diameter, and, say, forty feet long. And you want to prop one end of that pipe up about thirty-five or forty feet off the ground. And then you want a revolving belt—just work it with the waste steam from the engine—a revolving belt with a revolving chair in it. I am to sit in that chair, and have a Chinaman down there to fill up the bucket with sand, and pass it up as I come around and I am just to soar up there and tilt it into that pipe, and there you are. It is as easy as rolling off a log." You never saw a man so overcome with admiration—so overwhelmed. Before he knew what he was about he discharged me. He said I had too much talent to be fooling away my time in a quartz mill.

If you will permit me, I would like to illustrate the ups and downs of fortune in the mining country with just a little personal experience of my own. I had a cabin mate by the name of Higbie—a splendid good fellow. One morning the camp was thrown into a fearful state of excitement for the "Wide West" had struck a lead black with native silver and yellow with gold. The butcher had been dunning us a week or two. Higbie went up and brought a handful away and he sat studying and examining it, now and then soliloquizing in this manner: "That stuff never came out of the Wide West in the world." I told him it did, because I saw them hoist it out of the shaft. Higbie went away by himself, and came back in a couple of hours perfectly overcome with excitement. He came in, closed the door, went and looked out of the window to make sure there was nobody in the neighborhood, and said to me, "We are worth a million of dollars. The Wide West be hanged—that's a blind lead." Said I: "Higbie, are you *really* in earnest? Say it again: say it strong, Higbie." He replied: "Just as sure as I am standing here, it's a blind lead. We're rich." Poverty had vanished and we could buy that town and pay for it, and six more just like it. A blind lead is one that doesn't crop out above the ground like an ordinary quartz lead. The Wide West had simply tapped it in their shaft and we had discovered it. It belonged to us. It was our property and there wouldn't anybody in the camp dispute that fact. We took into partnership the foreman of the Wide West, and the Wide West had to stop digging. We were the lions of Esmerelda. People wanted to lend us money; other people wanted to sell us village lots on time; and the butcher brought us meat enough for a barbecue and went away without his pay.

Now there is a rule that a certain amount of work must be done on a new claim within the first ten days, or the claim is forfeited to anyone who may first take it up. Now I was called away to nurse an old friend who was dangerously ill at the Nine-Mile Ranch, and I just wrote a note and threw it into the window telling Higbie where I was gone. The fellow I went to nurse was an irascible sort of fellow, and while carrying him from the vapor bath I let my end of him fall, we had a quarrel and I started for home. When I reached there, I saw a cast concourse of people over at the claim and the thought struck me that we were richer than ever, probably worth two million certain. Presently I met Higbie looking like a ghost, and says I: "What on earth is the matter?" "Well," he says, "you didn't do the work on the mine. I depended on you. The foreman's mother dying in California, he didn't do the work, our claim is forfeited and we are ruined. We haven't a cent." We went home to the cabin. I looked down at the floor. There was my note, and beside it was a note from Higbie, telling me that he was going away to look for another mine which wouldn't have amounted to anything even if he had found it, in comparison with our claim.

It don't seem possible that there could be three as big fools in one small town, but we were there, and I was one of them. For once in my life I was absolutely a millionaire for just ten days by the watch. I was just ready to go into all kinds of dissipation and I am really thankful that this was a chapter in the history of my life, although at the time of course I did a great deal of weeping and gnashing my teeth. When I lost that million my heart was broken and I wanted to pine away and die, but I couldn't borrow money to live on while I did so, and I had to give that up. Everything appeared to go against me. Of course I might have suicided but that was kind of disagreeable.

I had written a few letters for the press, and just in the nick of time I received a letter from the Virginia City *Daily Enterprise* offering me $25 a week to go and be a reporter on that paper. I could hardly believe it, but this was no time for foolishness and I was in for anything. I never had edited anything, but if I had been offered the job of translating Josephus from the original Hebrew I should have taken it. If I had translated Josephus I would have thrown in as many jokes as I could for the money, and make him readable. I would have had a variety, if I had to write him all up new.

Well, I walked that 130 miles in pretty quick time and took the berth.

Have you ever considered what straits reporters are sometimes pushed to in furnishing the public with news? Why, the first day items were so scarce, I couldn't find an item anywhere, and just as I was on the verge of despair, as luck would have it there came in a lot of emigrants with their wagon trains. They had been fighting with the Indians and got the worst of it. I got the names of their killed and wounded, and then by and by there was another train came it. They hadn't had any trouble and of course I was disappointed, but I did the best I could under the circumstances. I cross-questioned the boss emigrant and found that they were going right on through and wouldn't come back to make trouble, so I got his list of names and added to my killed and wounded, and I got ahead of all the other papers. I put that wagon train through the bloodiest Indian fight ever seen on the plains. They came out of that conflict covered with glory. The chief editor said he didn't want any better reporter than I was. I said: "You just bring on your Indians and fetch out your emigrants, leave me alone, and I will make the fur fly. I will hang a scalp on every sagebrush between here and the Missouri border."

That was all first-rate, but by and by items got low again and I was downhearted. I was miserable, because I couldn't strike an item. At last fortune favored me again. A couple of dear delightful desperadoes got into a row right before me and one of them shot the other. I stepped in right up there and got the victim to give me his last words exclusively for the *Enterprise*, and I added some more to them so as to be sure to get ahead of the other papers, and then I turned to the desperado. Said I, "You are a stranger to me, sir, but you have done me a favor which I can never sufficiently thank you for. I shall ever regard you as a benefactor." And I asked him if he could lend me a half a dollar. We always borrowed a piece whenever we could—it was a public custom. The thought then struck me that I could raise a mob and hang on to the other desperado, but the officers got ahead of me and took him into custody. They were down on us and would always do any little mean thing like that, to spite us. And so I was fairly launched in literature, in the business of doing good. I love to do good. It is our duty. I think when a man does good all the time his conscience is so clear. I like to do right and be good, though there is a deal more fun in the other thing.

Now you see by my sort of experience a man may go to bed at night not worth a cent and wake up in the morning to find himself immensely wealthy, and very often he is a man who has a vast cargo of ignorance. To illustrate my point I will give you a story about a couple of those fresh nabobs whose names were Colonels Jim and Jack. Colonel Jim had seen considerable of the world, but Colonel Jack was raised down in the backwoods of Arkansas. These gentlemen after their good luck determined on a pleasure trip to New York; so they went to San Francisco, took a steamer, and in due time arrived in the great metropolis.

While passing along the street, Colonel Jack's attention was distracted by the hacks and splendid equipages he saw, and he says: "Well I've heard about these carriages all my life and I mean to have a ride in one. I don't care what it costs." So Colonel Jim stepped to the edge of the sidewalk and offered a handsome carriage. Colonel Jack says: "No, you don't. None of your cheap turnouts for me. I'm here to have a good time, and money's no object. I'm going to have the best rig this country affords. You stop that yellow one there with the pictures on it." So they got into the empty omnibus and sat down. Colonel Jack says: "Well, ain't it gay? Ain't it nice? Windows and pictures and cushions, till you can't rest. What would the boys think of this if they could see us cut such a swell in New York? I wish they could see us. What is the name of this?" Colonel Jim told him it was a barouche.

After a while he poked his head out in front and said to the driver, "I say, Johnny, this suits *me*. We want this shebang all day. Let the horses go." The driver loosened the strap and passed his hand in for the fare. Colonel Jack, thinking that he wanted to shake hands, shook him heartily and said, "You understand me. You take care of me and I'll take care of you." He put a twenty-dollar gold piece into the driver's hand. The driver says, "I can't change that." Colonel Jack replied, "Put it into your pocket, I don't want any change. We're going to ride it out."

In a few minutes the bus stopped and a young lady got in. Colonel Jack stared at her. Pretty soon she got out her money to pay the driver. Colonel Jack says, "Put up your money, Miss, you're perfectly welcome to ride here just as long as you want to, but this barouche is chartered and we can't let you pay." Soon an old lady got in. Colonel Jack told her to "sit down. Don't be at all uneasy, everything is paid for and as free as if you were in your own turnout, but you can't pay a cent." Pretty soon two or three gentlemen got in, and ladies with children. Colonel Jack says, "Come right along. Don't mind us. Free blowout." By and by the crowd filled all the seats and were standing up while the others climbed up on top. He nudged the Colonel Jim and says, "Colonel, what kind of cattle do they have here? If this don't bang anything I ever saw. Ain't they friendly, and so awful cool about it, but they ain't sociable." But I related enough of that circumstance to illustrate the enormous simplicity of those unfledged biddies of fortune.

I reported on that morning newspaper three years, and it was pretty hard work. But I enjoyed its attractions. Reporting is the best school in the world to get a knowledge of human beings, human nature, and human ways. A nice gentleman reporter—I make no references—is well treated by everybody. Just think of the wide range of his acquaintanceship, his experience of life and society. No other occupation brings a man into such familiar sociable relations with all grades and classes of people. The last thing at night—midnight—he goes browsing around after items among police and jailbirds, in the lockup, questioning the prisoners, and making pleasant and lasting friendships with some of the worst people on earth. And the very next evening he gets himself up regardless of expense, puts on all the good clothes his friends have got—goes and takes dinner with the Governor, or the Commander in Chief of the District, the United States Senator, and some more of the upper crust of society. He is on good terms with all of them, and is present at every public gathering, and has easy access to every variety of people. Why, I breakfasted almost every morning with the Governor, dined with the principal clergyman, and slept in the station house.

A reporter has to lie a little, of course, or they would discharge him. That is the only drawback to the profession. This is why I left it. I am different from Washington; I have a higher and grander standard of principle. Washington could not lie, I *can* lie but *won't*. Reporting is fascinating, but then it is distressing to have to lie so. Lying is bad—lying is very bad. Every individual in this house knows that by experience. I think that for a man to tell a lie when he can't make anything by it, is wrong.

When I finished reporting on that paper they made me chief editor. I lasted just a week. I edited that paper six days, and then I had five duels on my hands. I wouldn't have minded that if it had been the custom for those other people to challenge me. Then I would have simply declined with thanks. But it was not so. If you abused a man in the paper, if you called him names—they had no rights there such as we have—if the man didn't like it, you had to challenge him, and shoot him. Of course I didn't want to do this, but the publisher said it was the custom—society must be protected. If I could not do the duties of my position, he would have to hire somebody else.

I didn't mind the first three or four men; but the other man—I was after him. I knew he didn't want to fight, so I was going to make all the reputation out of him I could. He got touched at something I said about him—I don't know what it was now—I called him a thief, perhaps. He fought very shy of me at first, and so I plied him with bloodthirsty challenges all the more. At last he began to take an interest in this thing. It seemed as though he really was going to enter into it at last. All our boys were delighted at the prospect, but I was not. This was not a turn I was expecting in things.

I had taken for my second a fiery, peppery little fellow, named Steve, full of fight and anxious to have this thing fixed up right away. He took me over into a little ravine beyond the town to practice. It was the custom to fight with Colt's heavy revolvers at five steps. We borrowed a stable door for a mark from a gentleman who was absent. We set up that stable door, and then we propped a fence rail up against the middle to represent my antagonist, and put a squash on it to represent his head. He was a very light thin man, *very* thin—the poorest kind of material for a duel—you could not expect to do anything with a scattering shot at all. But he made a splendid line shot, and it was the line that I practiced on principally.

But there was no success about it. I could not hit the rail, and there was no need that I should hit the rail; the rail did not really represent him. It was a little too thin and narrow. But the squash was all right. Well, I could not hit the rail, and I could not hit the squash, and, finally, when I found I could not hit the door, either, I got a little discouraged. But when I noticed that I crippled one of the boys occasionally, I thought it was not so bad—I was dangerous with a pistol, but not reliable.

Finally we heard some shooting going on over in the other ravine. We knew what that meant. The other party was practicing, I didn't feel comfortable. They might straggle over the ridge, and see what was going on, and when they saw no bullet hold in the barn door, it would be too much encouragement for them. Just then a little bird, a little larger than a sparrow, lit on the sagebrush near by. Steve whipped out his revolver and shot its head off. The boys picked up the bird, and we were talking about it, when the other dueling party came over the ridge, and came down to see what was going on. When the second saw the bird he says, "How far off was that?" Steve said about thirty steps. "Who did that?" "Why, Twain, man, of course." "Did he, indeed! Can he do that often?" "Well, he can do that about four times in five."

I knew that little rascal was lying, but I didn't like to tell him so. I was one of those kind of men that don't like to be too frank or too familiar in a matter like that, so I didn't say anything. But it was a comfort to see those fellows' under jaws drop; to see them turn blue about the gills and look sick. They went off, and got their man, and took him home, and when I got home I found a little note from those parties, peremptorily declining the fight. How sore the boys were! How indignant they were! And so was I! But I was not distressed about it. I thought I could stand it, perhaps.

Well, I was out of that scrape, and I didn't want to get into any more of them. I turned the other four duels over to Steve, who wanted them. But when those people found out afterward that he did that shooting, he didn't get any good out of his duel. They wouldn't fight him.

All that was in my younger days, when I didn't know much—which I do now. I didn't know any better then, but now I am bitterly opposed to dueling. I think that dueling is immoral, and has a bad tendency, and I think it is every man's duty to frown down and discourage dueling. I do. I discourage it on all occasions. If a man were to challenge me now, I would go and take that man by the hand, and lead him to a quiet, private room—and kill him!

Ladies and gentlemen, after thanking you heartily for the attention you have given me this evening, I desire to wish you a very pleasant good night, and at the same time assure you earnestly that I have told nothing but the truth, and I have hardly exaggerated that.

"On Speech-Making Reform"

Like many another well-intentioned man, I have made too many speeches. And like other transgressors of this sort, I have from time to time reformed; binding myself, by oath, on New Year's Days, to never make another speech. I found that a new oath holds pretty well; but that when it is become old, and frayed out, and damaged by a dozen annual retyings of its remains, it ceases to be serviceable; any little strain will snap it. So, last New Year's Day I strengthened my reform with a money penalty; and made that penalty so heavy that it has enabled me to remain pure from that day to this. Although I am falling once more now, I think I can behave myself from this out, because the penalty is going to be doubled ten days hence. I see before me and about me the familiar faces of many poor sorrowing fellow sufferers, victims of the passion for speech-making—poor sad-eyed brothers in affliction, who, fast in the grip of this fell, degrading, demoralizing vice, have grown weak with struggling, as the years drifted by, and at last have all but given up hope. To them I say, in this last final obituary of mine, don't give up—don't do it; there is still hope for you. I beseech you, swear one more oath, and back it up with cash. I do not say this to all, of course; for there are some among you who are past reform; some who, being long accustomed to success, and to the delicious intoxication of the applause which follows it, are too wedded to their dissipation to be capable now or hereafter of abandoning it. They have thoroughly learned the deep art of speech-making, and they suffer no longer from those misgivings and embarrassments and apprehension which are really the only things which ever make a speech-maker want to reform. They have learned their art by long observation and slowly compacted experience, so now they know, what they did not know at first, that the best and most telling speech is not the actual impromptu one, but the counterfeit of it; they know that speech is most worth listening to which has been carefully prepared in private and tried on a plaster cast, or an empty chair, or any other appreciative object that will keep quiet, until the speaker has got this matter and his delivery limbered up so that they will seem impromptu to an audience. The expert knows that. A touch of indifferent grammar flung in here and there, apparently at random, has a good effect—often restores the confidence of a suspicious audience. He arranges these errors in private; for a really random error wouldn't do any good; it would be sure to fall in the wrong place. He also leaves blanks here and there—leaves them where genuine impromptu remarks can be dropped in, of a sort that will add to the natural aspect of the speech without breaking its line of march. At the banquet, he listens to the other speakers, invents happy turns upon remarks of theirs, and sticks these happy turns into his blanks for impromptu use by and by when he shall be called up. When this expert rises to his feet, he looks around over the house with the air of a man who has just been strongly impressed by something. The uninitiated cannot interpret his aspect, but the initiated can.

They know what is coming. When the noise of the clapping and stamping has subsided, this veteran says: "Aware that the hour is late, Mr. Chairman, it was my intention to abide by a purpose which I framed in the beginning of the evening—to simply rise and return my duty and thanks, in case I should be called upon, and then make way for men more able, and who have come with something to say. But sir, I was so struck by General Smith's remark concerning the proneness of evil to fly upward, that"—etc.,etc.,etc.; and before you know it he has slidden [*sic*] smoothly along on his compliment to the general, and out of it and into his set speech, and you can't tell, to save you, where it was nor when it was that he made the connection. And that man will soar along, in the most beautiful way, on the wings of a practiced memory; heaving in a little decayed grammar here, and a little wise tautology there, and a little neatly counterfeited embarrassment yonder, and a little finely acted stumbling and stammering for a word—rejecting this word and that, and finally getting the right one, and fetching it out with ripping effect, and with the glad look of a man who has got out of a bad hobble entirely by accident, and wouldn't take a hundred dollars for that accident; and every now and then he will sprinkle you in one of those happy turns on something that has previously been said; and at last, with supreme art, he will catch himself, when in the very act of sitting down, and lean over the table and fire a parting rocket, in the way of an afterthought, which makes everybody stretch his mouth as it goes up, and dims the very stars in heaven when it explodes. And yet that man has been practicing that afterthought and that attitude for about a week.

Well, you can't reform that kind of a man. It's a case of Eli joined to his idols—let him alone. But there is one sort that can be reformed. That is the genuinely impromptu speaker. I mean the man who "didn't expect to be called upon, and isn't prepared"; and yet goes waddling and warbling along, just as if he thought it wasn't any harm to commit a crime so long as it wasn't premeditated. Now and then he says, "but I must not detain you longer"; every little while he says, "Just one word more and I am done"—but at these times he always happens to think of two or three more unnecessary things and so he stops to say them. Now that man has no way of finding out how long his windmill is going. He likes to hear it creak; and so he goes on creaking, and listening to it, and enjoying it, never thinking of the flight of time; and when he comes to sit down at last, and look under his hopper, he is the most surprised person in the house to see what a little bit of grist he has ground, and how unconscionably long he has been grinding it. As a rule, he finds that he hasn't said anything—a discovery which the unprepared man ought usually to make, and does usually make—and has the added grief of making it at second hand, too.

This is a man who can be reformed. And so can his near relative, who now rises out of my reconstructed past—the man who provisions himself with a single prepared bite, of a sentence of two, and trusts to luck to catch quails and manna as he goes along. This person frequently gets left. You can easily tell when he has finished his prepared bit and begun on the impromptu part. Often the prepared portion has been built during the banquet; it may consist of ten sentences, but it oftener consists of two—oftenest of all, it is but a single sentence; and it has seemed so happy and pat and bright and good that the creator of it, the person that laid it, has been sitting there cackling privately over it and admiring it and petting it and shining it up, and imagining how fine it is going to "go," when, of course, he ought to have been laying another one, and still another one; and maybe a dozen or basketful if it's a fruitful day; yes, and he is thinking that when he comes to hurl that egg at the house there is going to be such an electric explosion of applause that the inspiration of it will fill him instantly with ideas and clothe the ideas in brilliant language, and that an impromptu speech will result which will be infinitely finer than anything he could have deliberately prepared. But there are two damaging things which he is leaving out of the calculation: one is, the historical fact that a man is never called up as soon as he thinks he is going to be called up, and that every speech that is injected into the proceedings ahead of him gives his fires an added chance to cool; and the other thing which he is forgetting is that he can't sit there and keep saying that fine sentence of his over and over to himself, for three-quarters of an hour without by and by getting a trifle tired of it and losing somewhat of confidence in it.

When at last his chance comes and he touches off his pet sentence, it makes him sick to see how shamefacedly and apologetically he has done it; and how compassionate the applause is; and how sorry everybody feels; and then he bitterly thinks what a lie it is to call this a free country where none but the unworthy and the undeserving may swear. And at this point, naked and blind and empty, he wallows off into his *real* impromptu speech; stammers out three or four incredibly flat things, then collapses into his seat, murmuring, "I wish I was in"—he doesn't say where, because he doesn't. The stranger at his left says, "Your opening was very good"; stranger at his right says, "I liked your opening"; man opposite says, "Opening very good indeed—very good"; two or three other people mumble something about his opening. People always feel obliged to pour some healing thing on a crippled man, that way. They mean it for oil; they think it *is* oil; but the sufferer recognizes it for aquafortis.

"Post-Prandial Oratory"

In treating of this subject of post-prandial oratory, a subject which I have long been familiar with and may be called an expert in observing it in others, I wish to say that a public dinner is the most delightful thing in the whole world, to a guest. That is one fact. And here is another one: a public dinner is the most unutterable suffering in the whole world, to a guest. These two facts don't seem to jibe—but I will explain. Now at a public dinner when a man knows he is going to be called upon to speak, and is thoroughly well prepared—got it all by heart, and the pauses all marked in his head where the applause is going to come in—a public dinner is just heaven to that man. He won't care to be anywhere else than just where he is. But when at a public dinner it is getting way along toward the end of things, and a man is sitting over his glass of wine, or his glass of milk, according to the kind of banquet it is, in ever-augmenting danger of being called up, and isn't prepared, and knows he can never prepare with the thoughtless gander at his elbow bothering him all the time with exasperating talky-talk about nothing, that man is just as nearly in the other place as ever he wants to be. Why, it is a cruel situation. That man is to be pitied; and the very worst of it is that the minute he gets on his feet he *is* pitied.

Now he could stand the pity of ten people or a dozen, but there is no misery in the world that is comparable to the massed and solidified compassion of five hundred. Why, that wide Sahara of sympathizing faces completely takes the tuck out of him, makes a coward of him. He stands there in his misery, and stammers out the usual rubbish about not being prepared, and not expecting, and all that kind of folly, and he is wandering and stumbling and getting further and further in, and all the time unhappy, and at last he fetches out a poor, miserable, crippled joke, and in his grief and confusion he laughs at it himself and the others look sick; and then he slumps into his chair and wishes he was dead. He knows he is a defeated man, and so do the others.

Now to a humane person that is a heartrending spectacle. It is indeed. That sort of sacrifice ought to be stopped, and there is only one way to accomplish it that I can think of, and that is for a man to go always prepared, always loaded, always ready, whether he is likely to be called upon or not. You can't defeat that man, you can't pity him at all. My scheme is this, that he shall carry in his head a cut-and-dried and thoroughly and glibly memorized speech that will fit every conceivable public occasion in this life, fit it to a dot, and win success and applause every time. Now I have completed a speech of that kind, and I have brought it along to exhibit here as a sample.

Now, then, supposing a man with his cut-and-dried speech, this patent adjustable speech, as you may call it, finds himself at a granger gathering, or a wedding breakfast, or a theological disturbance or a political blowout, an inquest, or funeral anywhere in the world you choose to mention, and be suddenly called up, all he has got to do is to change three or four words in that speech, and make his delivery anguished and tearful, or chippy and facetious, or luridly and thunderously eloquent just as the occasion happens to call for, and just turn himself loose, and he is all right, but I will illustrate, and instead of explanations I will deliver that speech itself just enough times to make you see the possibilities.

We suppose that it is a granger gathering, and this man is suddenly called on; he comes up with some artful hesitancies and diffidence and repetitions, so as to give the idea that the speech is impromptu. Here, of course, after he has got used to delivering it, he can venture outside and make a genuine impromptu remark to start off with. For instance, if a distinguished person is present, he can make a complimentary reference to him, say to Mr. Depew. He could speak about his great talent or his clothes. Such a thing gives him a sort of opening, and about the time that audience is getting to pity that man, he opens his throttle valve and goes for those grangers. That person wants to be gorgeously eloquent; you want to fire the farmer's heart and start him from his mansard down to his cellar.

Now, this man is called up, and he says: "I am called up suddenly, sir, and am indeed not, not prepared to—to—I was not expecting to be called up, sir, but I will, with what effect I may, add my shout to the jubilations of this spirit-stirring occasion. Agriculture, sir, is, after all, the palladium of our economic liberties. By it—approximately speaking—we may be said to live, and move, and have our being. All that we have been, all that we are, all that we hope to be, was, is, and must continue to be, profoundly influenced by that sublimest of the mighty interests of man, thrice glorious agriculture! While we have life, while we have soul, and in that soul the sweet and hallowed sentiment of gratitude, let us with generous accord attune our voices to songs of praise, perennial outpourings of thanksgiving, for that most precious boon, whereby we physically thrive, whereby our otherwise sterile existence is made rich and strong, and grand and aspiring, and is adorned with a mighty and far-reaching and all-embracing grace, and beauty, and purity and loveliness! The least of us knows—the least of us feels—the humblest among us will confess that, whereas—but the hour is late, sir, and I will not detain you."

Now then, supposing it is not a granger gathering at all, but is a wedding breakfast; now, of course, that speech has got to be delivered in an airy, light fashion, but it must terminate seriously. It is a mistake to make it any other way. This person is called up by the minister of the feast and he says: "I am called up suddenly, sir, and am, indeed, not prepared to—to—I was not expecting to be called up, sir, but I will, with what effect I may, add my shout to the jubilations of this spirit-stirring occasion. Matrimony, sir, is, after all, the palladium of our domestic liberties. By it—approximately speaking—we may be said to live, and move, and acquire our being. All that we have been, all that we are, all that we hope to be, was, is, and must continue to be profoundly influenced by that sublimest of the mighty interests of man, thrice glorious matrimony! While we have life, while we have soul, and in that soul the sweet and hallowed sentiment of gratitude, let us with generous accord attune our voices to songs of praise, perennial outpourings of thanksgiving, for that most precious boon whereby we numerically thrive, whereby our otherwise sterile existence is made rich, and strong, and grand, and aspiring, and is adorned with mighty and far-reaching and all-embracing grace, and beauty, and purity and liveliness! The least of us knows—the least of us feels—the humblest among us will confess, that whereas—but the hour is late, sir, and I will not detain you."

Now, then, supposing that the occasion—I make one more illustration, so that you will always be perfectly safe, here or anywhere—supposing that this is an occasion of an inquest. This is a most elastic speech in a matter of that kind. Where there are grades of men you must observe them. At a private funeral of some friend you want to be just as mournful as you can, but in the case where you don't know the person, grade it accordingly. You want simply to be impressive. That is all. Now take a case halfway between, about No. 4½, somewhere about there, that is, an inquest on a second cousin, a wealthy second cousin. He has remembered you in the will. Of course all these things count. They all raise the grade a little, and—well, perhaps he hasn't remembered you. Perhaps he has left you a horse, an ordinary horse, a good enough horse, one that can go about three minutes, or perhaps a pair of horses. It may have been one pair of horses at hand, not two pair or two pair and a jack. I don't know whether you understand that, but there are people here—. Well, now then, this is a second cousin, and he knows all the circumstances. We will say that he has lost his life trying to save somebody from drowning. Well, he saved the mind-cure physician from drowning, he tried to save him, but he didn't succeed. Of course he wouldn't succeed; of course you wouldn't want him to succeed in that way and plan. A person must have some experience and aplomb and all that before he can save anybody from drowning of the mind-cure. I am just making these explanations here. A person can get so glib in a delivery of this speech, why by the time he has delivered it fifteen or twenty times he could go to any intellectual gathering in Boston even, and he would draw like a prizefight. Well, at the inquest of a second cousin under these circumstances, a man gets up with graded emotion and he says:

"I am called up suddenly, sir, and am, indeed, not prepared to—to—I was not expecting to be called up, sir, but I will, with what effect I may, add my shout—voice to the lamentations of this spirit-crushing occasion. Death, death, sir, is, after all, the palladium of our spiritual liberties. By it—approximately speaking—we may be said to live, and move and have our ending. All that we have been, all that we may be here, all that we hope to be, was, is, and must continue to be profoundly influenced by that sublimest of the mighty interests of man, thrice-sorrowful dissolution. While we have life, while we have soul, and in that soul the sweet and hallowed sentiment of gratitude, let us with generous accord attune our voices to songs of praise, perennial outpourings of thanksgiving, for that most precious boon by which we spiritually thrive, whereby our otherwise sterile existence is made rich, and strong, and grand, and aspiring, and is adorned with a mighty and far-reaching and all-embracing grace, and beauty and purity, and liveliness. The least of us knows—the least of us feels—the humblest among us will confess, that whereas—but the hour is late, sir, and I will not detain you."

The speech as used at a funeral may be used to prop up prohibition, and also anti-prohibition, without change, except to change the terms of sorrow to terms of rejoicing.

The speech as used at a granger meeting may be used in Boston at the sacred feast of baked beans without any alteration except to change agriculture—where it occurs in the second sentence—to "the baked bean," and to "bean culture" where it occurs in the fourth.

The agricultural speech becomes a prohibition speech by putting in that word and changing "economic" to moral, and "physically" to morally. It becomes a Democratic, Republican, Mugwump of other political speech by shoving in the party name and changing "economic" to political and "physically" to politically.

Any of these forms can be used at a New England Forefathers dinner. *They* don't care what you talk about, so long as it ain't so.

"Dinner Speech" (Whitefriars Club)

Mr. Chairman and Brethren of the Vow—in whatever the vow is: for although I have been a member of this club for five-and-twenty years, I don't know any more about what that vow is that Mr. Austin seems to. But whatever the vow is, I don't care what it is. I have made a thousand vows.

There is no pleasure comparable to making a vow in the presence of one who appreciates that vow, in the presence of men who honor and appreciate you for making the vow, and the men who admire you for making the vow.

There is only one pleasure higher than that, and that is to get outside and break the vow. A vow is always a pledge of some kind or other for the protection of your own morals and principles or somebody else's, and generally, by the irony of fate, it is for the protection of your own morals.

Hence we have pledges that make us eschew tobacco or wine, and while you are taking the pledge there is a holy influence about that makes you feel you are reformed, and that you can never be so happy again in this world until—you get outside and take a drink.

I had forgotten that I was a member of this club—it is so long ago. But now I remember that I was here five-and-twenty years ago, and that I was then at a dinner of the Whitefriars Club, and it was in those old days when you had just made two great finds. All London was talking about nothing else than that they had found Livingstone, and that the lost Sir Roger Tichborne had been found—and they were trying him for it.

And at the dinner, Chairman, __________ (I do not know who he was)—failed to come to time. The gentleman who had been appointed to pay me the customary compliments and to introduce me forgot the compliments, and did not know what they were.

And George Augustus Sala came in at the last moment, just when I was about to go without compliments altogether. And that man was a gifted man.

They just called on him instantaneously, while he was going to sit down, to introduce the stranger, and Sala made one of those marvelous speeches which he was capable of making. I think no man talked so fast as Sala did. One did not need wine while he was making a speech. The rapidity of his utterance made a man drunk in a minute. An incomparable speech was that, an impromptu speech, and an impromptu speech is a seldom thing, and he did it so well.

He went into the whole history of the United States, and made it entirely new to me. He filled it with episodes and incidents that Washington never heard of, and he did it so convincingly that although I knew none of it happened, from that day to this I do not know any history but Sala's.

I do not know anything so sad as a dinner where you are going to get up and say something by and by, and you do not know what it is. You sit and wonder and wonder what the gentleman is going to say who is going to introduce you. You know that if he says something severe, that if he will deride you, or traduce you, or do anything of that kind, he will furnish you with a text, because anybody can get up and talk against that.

Anybody can get up and straighten out his character. But when a gentleman gets up and merely tells the truth about you, what can you do?

Mr. Austin has done well. He has supplied so many texts that I will have to drop out a lot of them, and that is about as difficult as when you do not have any text at all. Now, he made a beautiful and smooth speech without any difficulty at all, and I could have done that if I had gone on with the schooling with which I began. I see here a gentleman on my left who was my master in the art of oratory more than twenty-five years ago.

When I look upon the inspiring face of Mr. Depew, it carried me a long way back. An old and valued friend of mine is he, and I saw his career as it came along, and it has reached pretty well up to now, when he, by another miscarriage of justice, is a United States Senator. But those were delightful days when I was taking lessons in oratory.

My other master—the Ambassador—is not here yet. Under those two gentlemen I learned to make after-dinner speeches, and it was charming.

You know the New England dinner is the great occasion on the other side of the water. It is held every year to celebrate the landing of the Pilgrims. Those Pilgrims were a lot of people who were not needed in England, and you know they had great rivalry, and they were persuaded to go elsewhere, and they chartered a ship called *Mayflower* and set sail, and I have heard it said that they pumped the Atlantic Ocean through that ship sixteen times.

They fell in over there with the Dutch from Rotterdam, Amsterdam, and a lot of other places with profane names, and it is from hat gang that Mr. Depew is descended.

On the other hand, Mr. Choate is descended from those Puritans who landed on a bitter night in December. Every year those people used to meet at a great banquet in New York, and those masters of mind in oratory had to make speeches. It was Doctor Depew's business to get up there and apologize for the Dutch, and Mr. Choate had to get up later and explain the crimes of the Puritans, and grand, beautiful times we used to have.

It is curious that after that long lapse of time I meet the Whitefriars again, some looking as young and fresh as in the old days, others showing a certain amount of wear and tear, and here, after all this time, I find one of the masters of oratory and the others named in the list.

And here we three meet again as exiles on one pretext of another, and you will notice that while we are absent there is a pleasing tranquility in America—a building up of public confidence. We are doing the best we can for our country, and we never serve it to greater advantage than when we get out of it.

But impromptu speaking—that is what I was trying to learn. That is a difficult thing. I used to do it in this way. I used to begin about a week ahead, and write out my impromptu speech and get it by heart. Then I brought it to the New England dinner printed on a piece of paper in my pocket, so that I could pass it to the reporters all cut and dried, and in order to do an impromptu speech as it should be done you have to indicated the places for pauses and hesitations. I put them all in it. And then you want the applause in the right places.

When I got to the place where it should come in, if it did not come in I did not care, but I had it marked on the paper. And these masters of mind used to wonder why it was my speech came out in the morning in the first person, while theirs went through the butchery of synopsis.

I do that kind of speech (I mean an offhand speech), and do it well, and make no mistake, in such a way to deceive the audience completely and make that audience believe it is an impromptu speech—that is art.

I was frightened out of it at last by an experience of Doctor Hayes. He was a sort of Nansen of that day. He had been to the North Pole, and it made him celebrated. He had even seen the polar bear climb the pole.

He had made one of those magnificent voyages such as Nansen made, and in those days when a man did anything which greatly distinguished him for the moment he had to come on to the lecture platform and tell all about it.

Doctor Hayes was a great, magnificent creature like Nansen, superbly built. He was to appear in Boston. He wrote his lecture out, and it was his purpose to read it from manuscript; but in an evil hour he concluded that it would be a good thing to preface it with something rather handsome, poetical, and beautiful that he could get off by heart and deliver as if it were the thought of the moment.

He had not had my experience, and could not do that. He came on the platform, held his manuscript down, and began with a beautiful piece of oratory. He spoke something like this:

"When a lonely human being, a pigmy in the midst of the architecture of nature, stands solitary on those icy waters and looks abroad to the horizon and sees mighty castles and temples of eternal ice raising up their pinnacles tipped by the pencil of the departing sun—"

Here a man came across the platform and touched him on the shoulder, and said: "One minute." And then to the audience:
"Is Mrs. John Smith in the house? Her husband has slipped on the ice and broken his leg."

And you could see the Mrs. John Smiths get up everywhere and drift out of the house, and it made great gaps everywhere. Then Doctor Hayes began again: "When a lonely man, a pigmy in the architecture—" The janitor came in again and shouted: "It is not Mrs. John Smith! It is Mrs. John Jones!"

Then all the Mrs. Joneses got up and left. Once more the speaker started, and was in the midst of the sentence when he was interrupted again, and the result was that the lecture was not delivered. But the lecturer interviewed the janitor afterward in a private room, and of the fragments of that janitor they took "twelve basketsful."

Now, I don't want to sit down just in this way. I have been talking with so much levity that I have said no serious thing, and you are really no better or wiser, although Robert Buchanan has suggested that I am a person who deals in wisdom. I have said nothing which would make you better than when you came here.

I should be sorry to sit down without having said one serious word which you can carry home and relate to your children and the old people who are not able to get away.

And this is just a little maxim which has saved me from many a difficulty and many a disaster, and in times of tribulation and uncertainty has come to my rescue, as it shall to yours if you observe it as I do day and night.

I always use it in an emergency, and you can take it home as a legacy from me, and it is: "When in doubt, tell the truth."

"The Babies: As They Comfort Us in Our Sorrows, Let Us Not Forget Them in Our Festivities"

I like that. We haven't all had the good fortune to be ladies; we haven't all been generals, or poets, or statesmen; but when the toast works down to the babies, we stand on common ground, for we've all been babies. It is a shame that for a thousand years the world's banquets have utterly ignored the baby—as if *he* didn't amount to anything! If you gentlemen will stop and think a minute—if you will go back fifty or a hundred years, to your early married life, and recontemplate your first baby, you will remember that he amounted to a good deal, and even something over. You soldiers all know that when that little fellow arrived at family headquarters, you had to hand in your resignation. He took entire command. You became his lackey—his mere body servant, and you had to stand around, too. He was not a commander who made allowances for time, distance, weather, or anything else—you had to execute his order whether it was possible or not. And there was only one form of marching in his manual of tactics, and that was the double-quick. He treated you with every sort of insolence and disrespect, and the bravest of you didn't dare to say a word.

You could face the death storm at Donelson and Vicksburg, and give back blow for blow; but when he clawed your whiskers, and pulled your hair, and twisted your nose, you had to take it. When the thunders of war were sounding in your ears, you set your face toward the batteries and advanced with steady tread; but, when he turned on the terrors of his war whoop, you advanced in the other direction—and mighty glad of the chance, too. When he called for soothing syrup, did you venture to throw out any side remarks about certain services being unbecoming an officer and a gentleman? No. You got up and *got* it. When he ordered his pap bottle, and it wasn't warm, did you talk back? Not you. You went to work and *warmed* it. You even descended so far in your menial office as to take a suck at that warm, insipid stuff yourself, just to see if it was right—three parts water to one of milk, a touch of sugar to modify the colic, and a drop of peppermint to kill those infernal hiccups. I can taste that stuff yet.

And how many things you learned, as you went along! Sentimental young folks still take stock in that beautiful old saying that when the baby smiles in his sleep, it is because the angels are whispering to him. Very pretty, but too thin—simply wind on the stomach, my friends! If the baby proposed to take a walk at the usual hour—half-past two in the morning—didn't you rise up promptly and remark—with a mental addition which wouldn't improve a Sunday school book much—that was the very thing you were about to propose yourself? Oh, you were under good discipline. And as you went fluttering up and down the room in your undress uniform, you not only prattled undignified baby talk, but even tuned up your martial voices and tried to *sing!*—"Rock-a-by baby in the tree top," for instance. And what an affliction for the neighbors, too—for it isn't everybody within a mile around that likes military music at three in the morning. And when you had been keeping this sort of thing up two or three hours, and your little velvet-head intimated that nothing suited him like exercise and noise, and proposed to fight it out on that line if it took all night—what did you do? You simply *went* on till you dropped in the last ditch.

The idea that a *baby* doesn't amount to anything! Why *one* baby is just a house and front yard full by itself. *One* baby can furnish more business than you and your whole Interior Department can attend to. He is enterprising, irrepressible, brim full of lawless activities. Do what you please, you can't make him stay on the reservation. Sufficient unto the day is one baby—as long as you are in your right mind don't you ever pray for twins. Twins amount to a permanent riot; and there ain't any real difference between triplets and an insurrection.

Yes, it was high time for a toastmaster to recognize the importance of the babies. Think what is in store for the present crop! Fifty years from now we shall all be dead—I trust—and then this flag, if it still survive—and let us hope it may—will be floating over a Republic numbering 200,000,000 souls, according to the settled laws of our increase; our present schooner of State will have grown into a political leviathan—a *Great Eastern*—and the cradled babies of today will be on deck. Let them be well trained, for we are going to leave a big contract on their hands. Among the three or four million cradles now rocking in the land are some which this nation would preserve for ages as sacred things, if we could know which ones they are. In one of these cradles the unconscious Farragut of the future is at this moment *teething*—think of it!—and putting in a world of dead earnest, unarticulated and perfectly justifiable profanity over it, too; in another, the future renowned astronomer is blinking at the shining Milky Way, with but a languid interest—poor little chap!—and wondering what has become of that other one they call the wet nurse; in another the future great historian is lying—and doubtless he will continue to lie until his earthly mission is ended; in another the future President is busying himself with no profounder problem of state than what the mischief has become of his hair so early, and in a mighty array of other cradles there are now some sixty thousand future office-seekers getting ready to furnish him occasion to grapple with that same old problem a second time.

And in still one more cradle, somewhere under the flag, the future illustrious Commander in Chief of the American armies is so little burdened with his approaching grandeurs and responsibilities as to be giving his whole strategic mind, at this moment, to trying to find out some way to get his own big toe into his mouth—an achievement which, meaning no disrespect, the illustrious guest of this evening turned *his* whole attention some fifty-six years ago. And if the child is but a prophecy of the man, there are mighty few who will doubt that he *succeeded*.

"Dinner Speech" (Whittier's Birthday)

Mr. Chairman: This is an occasion peculiarly meet for the digging up of pleasant reminiscences concerning literary folk; therefore I will drop lightly into history myself. Standing here on the shore of the Atlantic and contemplating certain of its biggest literary billows, I am reminded of a thing which happened to me some fifteen years ago, when I had just succeeded in stirring up a little Nevadian literary ocean puddle myself, whose spume flakes were beginning to blow Californiawards. I started an inspection tramp through the southern mines of California. I was callow and conceited, and I resolved to try the virtue of my *nom de plume*. I very soon had an opportunity. I knocked at a miner's lonely log cabin in the foothills of the Sierras just at nightfall. It was snowing at the time. A jaded, melancholy man of fifty, barefooted, opened to me. When he heard my *nom de plume*, he looked more dejected than before. He let me in—pretty reluctantly, I thought—and after the customary bacon and beans, black coffee and a hot whiskey, I took a pipe. This sorrowful man had not said three words up to this time. Now he spoke up and said in the voice of one who is secretly suffering, "You're the fourth—I'm a-going to move." "The fourth what?" said I. "The fourth littery man that's been here in twenty-four hours—I'm a-going to move." "You don't tell me!" said I; "Who were the others?" "Mr. Longfellow, Mr. Emerson and Mr. Oliver Wendell Holmes—dad fetch the lot!"

You can easily believe I was interested. I supplicated—three hot whiskies did the rest—and finally the melancholy miner began. Said he:

"They came here just at dark yesterday evening, and I let them in, of course. Said they were going to Yosemite. They were a rough lot—but that's nothing—everybody looks rough that travels afoot. Mr. Emerson was a seedy little bit of a chap—red-headed. Mr. Holmes was as fat as a balloon—he weighed as much as three hundred, and had double chins all the way down to his stomach. Mr. Longfellow was built like a prizefighter. His head was cropped and bristly—like as if he had a wig made of hair brushes. His nose lay straight down his face, like a finger, with the end joint tilted up. They had been drinking—I could see that. And what queer talk they used! Mr. Holmes inspected the cabin, then he took me by the buttonhole and says he:

Through the deep caves of thought
I hear a voice that sings:
Build thee more stately mansions,
O my Soul!

"Says I, 'I can't afford it, Mr. Holmes, and moreover I don't want to.' Blamed if I liked it pretty well, either, coming from a stranger that way! However, I started to get out my bacon and beans, when Mr. Emerson came and looked on a while, and then *he* takes me aside by the buttonhole and says:

Give me agates for my meat;
Give me cantharides to eat;
From air and ocean bring me foods,
From all zones and latitudes.

"Says I, 'Mr. Emerson. if you'll excuse me, this ain't no hotel.' You see it sort of riled me—I warn't used to the ways of littery swells. But I went out a-sweating over my work, and next comes Mr. Longfellow and buttonholes me, and interrupts me. Says he:

Honor be to Mudjekeewis!
You shall hear how Pau-Puk-Kee-wis—

"But I broke in, and says I, 'Begging your pardon, Mr. Longfellow, if you'll be so kind as to hold your yawp for about five minutes, and let me get this grub ready, you'll do me proud.' Well sir, after they'd filled up, I set out the jug. Mr. Holmes looks at it, and then he fires up all of a sudden and yells:

Flash out a stream of blood-red wine!
For I would drink to other days.

"By George, I was getting kind of worked up. I don't deny it, I was getting kind of worked up. I turns to Mr. Holmes, and says I, 'Looky here, my fat friend. I'm a-running this shanty, and if the court knows herself, you'll take whiskey straight or you'll go dry!' Them's the very words I said to him. Now I didn't want to sass such famous littery people, but you see they kind of forced me. There ain't nothing onreasonable 'bout me; I don't mind a passel of guests a-tread'n on my tail three or four times, but when it comes to *standin'* on it, it's different, and if the court knows herself, you'll take whiskey straight or you'll go dry! Well, between drinks they'd swell around the cabin and strike attitudes and spout. Says Mr. Longfellow:

> This is the forest primeval.

"Says Mr. Emerson:

> Here once the embattled farmers stood,
> And fired the shot heard round the world.

"Says I, 'Oh, blackguard the premises as much as you want to—it don't cost you a cent.' Well, they went on drinking, and pretty soon they got out a greasy old deck and went to playing cutthroat euchre at ten cents a corner—on trust. I begun to notice some pretty suspicious things. Mr. Emerson dealt, looked at his hand, shook his head, says:

> I am the doubter and the doubt—

and calmly bunched the hands and went to shuffiing for a new layout. Says he:

> They reckon ill who leave me out;
> They know not well the subtle ways
> I keep. I pass, and deal *again!*

"Hang'd if he didn't go ahead and do it, too! Oh, he was a cool one. Well, in about a minute, things were running pretty tight, but all of a sudden I see by Mr. Emerson's eye that he judged he had 'em. He had already corralled two tricks, and each of the others one. So now he kind of lifts a little, in his chair, and says:

> I tire of globes and aces!
> Too long the game is played!

—and down he fetched a right bower. Mr. Longfellow smiles as sweet as pie, and says:

Thanks, thanks to thee, my worthy friend,
For the lesson thou has taught.

—and dog my cats if he didn't come down with *another* right bower! Well, sir, up jumps Holmes a-war whooping, as usual, and says:

God help them if the tempest swings
The pine against the palm!

—and I wish I may go to grass if he didn't swoop down with *another* right bower! Emerson claps his hand on his bowie, Longfellow claps his on his revolver, and I went under a bunk. There was going to be trouble; but that monstrous Holmes rose up, wobbling his double chins, and says he, 'Order, gentlemen; the first man that draws, I'll lay down on him and smother him!" All quiet on the Potomac, you bet you!

"They were pretty how-come-you-so-now, and they begun to blow. Emerson says, 'The bulliest thing I ever wrote was "Barbara Frietchie."' Says Longfellow, 'It don't begin with my "Biglow Papers."' Says Holmes, 'My "Thanatopsis" lays over 'em both.' They mighty near ended in a fight. Then they wished they had some more company—and Mr. Emerson pointed at me and says:

Is yonder squalid peasant all
That this proud nursery could breed?

"He was a-whetting his bowie on his boot-so I let is pass. Well, sir, next they took it into their heads that they would like some music; so they made me stand up and sing 'When Johnny Comes Marching Home' till I dropped—at thirteen minutes past four this morning. That's what *I've* been through, my friend. When I woke at seven, they were leaving, thank goodness, and Mr. Longfellow had my only boots on, and his own under his arm. Says I, "Hold on there, Evangeline, what you going to do with *them?*" He says: 'Going to make tracks with 'em, because

Lives of great men all remind us
We can make our lives sublime;
And departing, leave behind us
Footprints on the sands of Time.

"As I said, Mr. Twain, you are the fourth in twenty-four hours—and I'm a-going to move—I ain't suited to a littery atmosphere."

I said to the miner, "Why, my dear sir, *these* were not the gracious singers to whom we and the world pay loving reverence and homage; these were imposters."

The miner investigated me with a calm eye for a while, then said he, "Ah—imposters, were they?—are *you?*" I did not pursue the subject; and since then I haven't traveled on my *nom de plume* enough to hurt. Such is the reminiscence I was moved to contribute, Mr. Chairman. In my enthusiasm I may have exaggerated the details a little, but you will easily forgive me that fault, since I believe it is the first time I have ever deflected from perpendicular fact on an occasion like this.

"Remarks" (Public Education Association)

I don't suppose that I am called here as an expert on education, or, at least, I should hope not, and when I thank the president and members of society for asking me here at all, I do so with the distinct understanding that I am not expected to furnish information. I am incapable of it.

As I sat here looking around for an idea it struck me that I was called for two reasons. One was to do good to me, a poor unfortunate traveler on the world's wide ocean, by giving me a knowledge of the nature and scope of your society and letting me know that others beside myself have been of some use in the world. The second reason is that I am asked here to operate as a contrast—the contrast of an idle and lazy man in the company of 600 or 700 earnest, energetic women, and, further, to show by this contrast, the possibilities of education. Go on with your good work and you will receive the applause of the idle and lazy as well as the others.

Oh, I have a wild and vague and nebulous idea of the aims and objects of the society, and already I applaud. If I understood fully the grand scope of your organization I might raise my applause to a still higher key. Such as it is, it's genuine and there's plenty of it.

The president has just mentioned the fact that the society has won one great credit mark in the fact that it has been called upon for instruction by the Charter Revision Commission. The commission would not have made this request unless it had felt sure of being able to learn something of its counsels.

Reference has been made to the fact that the pictures of the New York schools have gone here and there throughout Europe for the instruction of foreign governments, and are now in the hands of Russia. Well, that was a compliment that I was not expecting for our educational system, because it has not been an hour since I was reading a cable dispatch in one of the newspapers which began, "Russia proposes to retrench."

When one is not expecting a thunderbolt like that it is exciting. I thought, what a good thing for the whole world! "Russia has 30,000 soldiers in Manchuria," I said to myself, "and this dispatch means that she is going to take them out of there and send them back to their farms to live in peace. If Russia retrenches this way why shouldn't Germany and France follow suit? Why shouldn't all the foreign powers withdraw from China and leave her free to attend to her own business?"

Why should not China be free from the foreigners, who are only making trouble on her soil? If they would only all go home, what a pleasant place China would be for the Chinese!

As far as America is concerned we don't allow the Chinese to come here, and we would be doing the graceful thing to allow China to decide whether she will allow us to go there. China never wanted any foreigners, and when it comes to a settlement of the immigrant question I am with the Boxer every time.

The Boxer is a patriot; he is the only patriot China has. The Boxer believes in driving us out of his country. I wish him success. I am a Boxer myself, because I believe in driving the Chinaman out of this country. The Boxers on this side have won out. Why not give the Boxer on the other side a chance?

It occurred to me to finish that cablegram. The rest said: "Russia, in order to retrench, has resolved to withdraw the appropriation for public schools." Now, I never expected to see any humor in a cable dispatch from Russia. The worst thing about it is that the Russians themselves probably don't see any humor in it. The idea of a country concluding that the best way to save expenses is to cut off the common schools! We, who have been led to believe that out of the schools grows a nation's greatness, can hardly believe this tale.

It is curious to reflect how history repeats itself and how great minds all over the earth are sure at some time to alight on the same great idea. Now, this same Russian plan of retrenchment was brought up once in a township on the Mississippi River when I was a boy. The town was short of money and it was proposed to discontinue the common schools. At a meeting where the scheme was being discussed, an old farmer got up and said:

"I think it's a mistake to try and save money that way. It's not a real saving, for every time you stop a school you will have to build a jail. What you gain at one end you lose at the other. It's like feeding a dog on his own tail. It wouldn't fatten that dog."

This society is much wiser in its day and generation than the Emperor of Russia and all his people. That is not much of a compliment, but it's the best I've got in stock.

"Introducing Winston S. Churchill"

Mr. Churchill and I do not agree on the righteousness of the South African war, but that is of no consequence. There is no place where people all think alike—well, there is heaven; there they do, but let us hope it won't be so always.

For forty years I have been a self-appointed missionary, and have wrought zealously for my cause—the joining together of America and the motherland in bonds of friendship, esteem and affection—an alliance of the heart which should permanently and beneficently influence the political relations of the two countries. Wherever I have stood before a gathering of Americans of Englishmen, in England, India, Australia or elsewhere, I have urged my mission, and warmed it up with compliments to both countries and pointed out how nearly alike the two peoples are in character and spirit. They ought to be united.

Behold America, the refuge of the homeless, the hunted, the oppressed from everywhere (who can pay ten dollars, admission)—anyone except a Chinaman—standing up for human rights everywhere, even helping to make China admit the foreigner when she didn't want him, and to let him in free when she wanted to charge him fifty dollars if he was a harmless Christian or kill him if he was a missionary. And how England, mother of human liberty, uttered that great word, "the slave that sets his foot upon English soil is free" and with her strong hand made that gospel good in every acre of that vast Empire whose dominions girdle the globe; and how unselfishly England has wrought for the open door for all.

And how nobly and piously America also has stood for that same door in all cases where it wasn't her own; and how generous we have been, and how generous England has been in not requiring fancy rates for extinguishing missionaries, the way Germany does, but willing to take produce for them—firecrackers and tea—while Germany has to have territory and cash, and monuments and any other loot that's in reach—and memorial churches, and has thus made true changes of heart and regeneration, and the other details of German trinity so expensive that China won't be able to afford German missionaries any more till she gets in better shape financially; and how self-respectingly England and America have refrained from imitating German bluster, German rapacity, the mailed fist with a burglar's jimmy in it, and the investing mouth above it which alternately chortles bargain counter piety and "no quarter" according to the state of the market; and how nobly (and shamefacedly) we both stood timorously by at Port Arthur and wept sweetly and sympathizingly and shone while France and Germany helped Russia to rob the Japanese; and how gallantly we went to the rescue of poor Cuba, friendless, despairing, borne down by centuries of bitter slavery, and broke off her chains and set her free—with approving England at our back in an attitude toward European powers which did us good service in those days, and we confess it now.

Yes, as a missionary I have sung the song of praise and still sing it; and yet I think that England sinned in getting into war in South Africa which she could have avoided without loss of credit or dignity—just as I think we have sinned in crowding ourselves into a war in the Philippines on the same terms.

Mr. Churchill will tell you about the war in South Africa, and he is competent—he fought and wrote through it himself. And he made a record there which would be a proud one for a man twice his age. By his father he is English, by his mother he is American—to my mind the blend which makes the perfect man. We are now on the friendliest terms with England. Mainly through my missionary efforts I suppose; and I am glad. We have always been kin: kin in blood, kin in religion, kin in representative government, kin in ideals, kin in just and lofty purposes; and now we are kin in sin, the harmony is complete, the blend is perfect, like Mr. Churchill himself, whom I now have the honor to present to you.

"Plymouth Rock and the Pilgrims"

I rise to protest. I have kept still for years, but really I think there is no sufficient justification for this sort of thing. What do you want to celebrate those people for?—those ancestors of yours, of 1620—the *Mayflower* tribe, I mean. What do you want to celebrate *them* for? Your pardon; the gentleman at my left assures me that you are not celebrating the Pilgrims themselves, but the landing of the Pilgrims at Plymouth Rock on the 22d of December. So you are celebrating their landing. Why, the other pretext was thin enough, but this is thinner than ever; the other was tissue, tinfoil, fish bladder, but this is gold leaf.

Celebrating their landing! What was there remarkable about it, I would like to know? What can you be thinking of? Why, those Pilgrims had been at sea three or four months. It was the very middle of the winter; it was as cold as death off Cape Cod, there. Why shouldn't they come ashore? If they hadn't landed there would be some reason in celebrating the fact. It would have been a case of monumental leatherheadedness which the world would not willingly let die. If it had been *you*, gentlemen, you probably wouldn't have landed, but you have no shadow of right to be celebrating, in your ancestors, gifts which they did not exercise, but only transmitted. Why, to be celebrating the mere landing of the Pilgrims—to be trying to make out that this most natural, and simple, and customary procedure was an extraordinary circumstance—a circumstance to be amazed at and admired, aggrandized and glorified, at orgies like this for two hundred and sixty years—hang it, a horse would have known enough to land; a horse—pardon again; the gentleman on my right assures me that it was not merely the landing of the Pilgrims that we are celebrating, but the Pilgrims themselves. So we have struck an inconsistency here—one says it was the landing, the other says it was the

Pilgrims. It is an inconsistency characteristic of your intractable and disputatious tribe, for you never agree about anything but Boston.

Well, then, what do you want to celebrate those Pilgrims for? They were a mighty hard lot—you know it. I grant you, without the slightest unwillingness, that they were a deal more gentle and merciful and just than were the peoples of Europe of that day; I grant you that they were better than their predecessors. But what of that?—that is nothing. People always progress. You are better than your fathers and grandfathers were (this is the first time I have ever aimed a measureless slander at the departed, for I consider such things improper). Yes, those among you who have not been in the penitentiary, if such there be, are better than your fathers and grandfathers were, but is that any sufficient reason for getting up annual dinners and celebrating you? No, by no means—by no means. Well, I repeat, those Pilgrims were a hard lot. They took good care of themselves, but they abolished everybody else's ancestors. I am a border ruffian from the state of Missouri. I am a Connecticut Yankee by adoption. I have the morals of Missouri and the culture of Connecticut, and that's the combination that makes the perfect man.

But where are my ancestors? Whom shall I celebrate? Where shall I find the raw material? My first American ancestor, gentleman, was an Indian—an early Indian. Your ancestors skinned him alive, and I am an orphan. Not one drop of my blood flows in that Indian's veins today. I stand here, lone and forlorn, without an ancestor. They skinned him! I do not object to that, if they needed his fur; but alive, gentlemen—alive! They skinned him alive—and before company! That is what rankles. Think how he must have felt; for he was a sensitive Indian and easily embarrassed. If he had been a bird, it would have been all right, and no violence done to his feelings, because he would have been considered "dressed." But he was not a bird, gentlemen, he was a man, and probably one of the most undressed men that ever was. I ask you to put yourselves in his place. I ask it as a favor; I ask it as a tardy act of justice; I ask it in the interest of fidelity to the traditions of your ancestors; I ask it that the world may contemplate, with vision unobstructed by disguising swallowtails and white cravats, the spectacle which the true New England Society ought to present. Cease to come to these annual orgies in this hollow modern mockery—the surplusage of raiment. Come in character; come in the summer grace, come in the unadorned simplicity, come in the free and joyous costume which your sainted ancestors provided for mine.

Later ancestors of mine were the Quakers, William Robinson, Marmaduke Stephenson, *et al*. Your tribe chased them out of the country for their religion's sake; promised them death if they came back, for your ancestors had forsaken the homes they loved, and braved the perils of the sea, the implacable climate, and the savage wilderness, to acquire that highest and most precious of boons, freedom for every man on this broad continent to worship according to the dictates of his own conscience—and they were not going to allow a lot of pestiferous Quakers to interfere with it. Your ancestors broke forever the chains of political slavery, and gave the vote to every man in this wide land, excluding none!—none except those who did not belong to the orthodox church. Your ancestors—yes, they were a hard lot; but, nevertheless, they gave us religious liberty to worship as they required us to worship, and political liberty to vote as the church required; and so I, the bereft one, I, the forlorn one, am here to do my best to help you celebrate them right.

The Quaker woman, Elizabeth Hooton, was an ancestress of mine. Your people were pretty severe with her—you will confess that. But, poor thing! I believe they changed her opinions before she died, and took her into their fold; and so we have every reason to presume that when she died she went to the same place which your ancestors to. It is a pity, for she was a good woman. Roger Williams was an ancestor of mine. I don't really remember what your people did with him, But they banished him to Rhode Island, anyway. And then, I believe, recognizing that this was really carrying harshness to an unjustifiable extreme, they took pity on him and burned him. They were a hard lot! All those Salem witches were ancestors of mine. Your people made it tropical for them. Yes, they did; by pressure and the gallows they made such a clean deal with them that there hasn't been a witch and hardly a halter in our family from that day to this, and that is 189 years. The first slave brought into New England out of Africa by your progenitors was an ancestor of mine—for I am of a mixed breed, an infinitely shaded and exquisite mongrel. I'm not one of your sham meerschaums that you can color in a week. No, my complexion is the patient art of eight generations. Well, in my own time, I had acquired a lot of my kin—by purchase, and swapping around, and one way and another—and was getting along very well. Then, with the inborn perversity of your lineage, you got up a war and took them all away from me. And so, again am I bereft, again am I forlorn; no drop of my blood flows in the veins of any living being who is marketable.

Oh my friends, hear me and reform! I seek your good, not mine. You have heard the speeches. Disband these New England societies—nurseries of a system of steadily augmenting laudation and hosannahing, which, if persisted in uncurbed, may some day in the remote future beguile you into prevaricating and bragging. Oh, stop, stop while you are still temperate in your appreciation of your ancestors! Hear me, I beseech you, get up an auction and sell Plymouth Rock! The Pilgrims were a simple and ignorant race. They had never seen any good rocks before, or at least any that were not watched, and so they were excusable for hopping ashore in frantic delight and clapping an iron fence around this one. But you, gentlemen, are educated; you are enlightened; you know that in the rich land of your nativity, opulent New England, overflowing with rocks, this one isn't worth, at the outside, more than thirty-five cents. Therefore, sell it, before it is injured by exposure, or at least throw it open to the patent medicine advertisements, and let it earn its taxes.

Yes, hear your true friend—your only true friend—list to his voice. Disband these societies, hotbeds of vice, of moral decay—perpetuators of ancestral superstition. Here on this board I see water, I see milk, I see the wild and deadly lemonade. These are but steps upon the downward path. Next we shall see tea, then chocolate, then coffee—hotel coffee. A few more years—all too few, I fear—mark my words, we shall have cider! Gentlemen, pause ere it be too late. You are on the broad road which leads to dissipation, physical ruin, moral decay, gory crime and the gallows! I beseech you, I implore you, in the name of your anxious friends, in the name of your suffering families, in the name of your impending windows and orphans, stop ere it be too late. Disband these New England societies, renounce these soul-blistering saturnalia, cease from varnishing the rusty reputations of your long-vanished ancestors—the super-high moral old ironclads of Cape Cod, the pious buccaneers of Plymouth Rock—go home, and try to learn to behave!

However, chaff and nonsense aside, I think I honor and appreciate your Pilgrim stock as much as you do yourselves, perhaps, and I endorse and adopt a sentiment uttered by a grandfather of mine once—a man of sturdy opinions, of sincere make of mind, and not given to flattery. He said: "People may talk as they like about that Pilgrim stock, but, after all's said and done, it would be pretty hard to improve on those people; and, as for me, I don't mind coming out flat-footed and saying there ain't any way to improve on them—except having them born in Missouri!"

"On Foreign Critics"

If I look harried and worn, it is not from an ill conscience. It is from sitting up nights to worry about the foreign critic. He won't concede that we have a civilization—a "real" civilization. Five years ago, he said we had never contributed anything to the betterment of the world. And now comes Sir Lepel Griffin, whom I had not suspected of being in the world at all, and says "there is not country calling itself civilized where one would not rather live than in America, except Russia." That settles it. That is, it settles it for Europe, but it doesn't make me any more comfortable than I was before.

What is a "real" civilization? Nobody can answer that conundrum. They have all tried. Then suppose we try to get at what it is not; and then subtract the what it is not from the general sum, and call the remainder "real" civilization—so as to have a place to stand on while we throw bricks at these people. Let us say, then, in broad terms, that any system which has in it any one of these things, to wit, human slavery, despotic government, inequality, numerous and brutal punishments for crimes, superstition almost universal, ignorance almost universal—is not a real civilization, and any system which has none of them, is.

If you grant these terms, one may then consider this conundrum: How old is real civilization? The answer is easy and unassailable. A century ago it had not appeared anywhere in the world during a single instant since the world was made. If you grant these terms—and I don't see why it shouldn't be fair, since civilization must surely mean the humanizing of a people, not a class—there is today but one real civilization in the world, and it is not yet thirty years old. We made the trip and hoisted its flag when we disposed of our slavery.

However, there are some partial civilizations scattered around over Europe—pretty lofty civilizations they are, too—but who begot them? What is the seed from which they sprang? Liberty and intelligence. What planted that seed? There are dates and statistics which suggest that it was the

American Revolution that planted it. When that revolution began, monarchy had been on trail some thousands of years, over there, and was a distinct and convicted failure, every time. It had never produced anything but a vast, a nearly universal savagery, with a thin skim of civilization on top, and the main part of that was nickel plate and tinsel. The French, imbruted and impoverished by centuries of oppression and official robbery, were a starving nation clothed in rags, slaves of an aristocracy of smirking dandies clad in unearned silks and velvet. It makes one's cheek burn to read of the laws of the time and realize that they were for human beings; realize that they originated in this world, and not in hell. Germany was unspeakable. In the Scottish lowlands the people lived in styes, and were human swine; in the highlands drunkenness was general, and it hardly smirched a young girl to have a family of her own. In England there was a sham liberty, and not much of that; crime was general; ignorance the same; poverty and misery were widespread; London fed a tenth of her population by charity; the law awarded the death penalty to almost every conceivable offense; what was called medical science by courtesy stood where it had stood for two thousand years; Tom Jones and Squire Western were gentlemen.

The printer's art had been known in Germany and France three and a quarter centuries, and in England three. In all that time there had not been a newspaper in Europe that was worthy the name. Monarchies had no use for that sort of dynamite. When we hoisted the banner of revolution and raised the first genuine shout for human liberty that had ever been heard, this was a newspaperless globe. Eight years later, there were six daily journals in London to proclaim to all the nations the greatest birth this world had ever seen. Who woke that printing press out of its trance of three hundred years? Let us be permitted to consider that we did it. Who summoned the French slaves to rise and set the nation free? We did it. What resulted in England and on the Continent? Crippled liberty took up its bed and walked. From that day to this its march has not halted, and please God it never will. We are called the nation of inventors. And we are. We could still claim that title and wear its loftiest honors, if we had stopped with the first thing we ever invented—which was human liberty. Out of that invention has come the Christian world's great civilization. Without it was impossible—as the history of all the centuries has proved. Well, then, who invented civilization? Even Sir Lepel Griffin ought to be able to answer that question. It looks easy enough. *We* have contributed nothing! Nothing hurts me like ingratitude.

Yes, the coveted verdict has been persistently withheld from us. Mr. Arnold granted that our whole people—including by especial mention "that immense class, the great bulk of the community," the wage and salary-earners—have liberty, equality, plenty to eat, plenty to wear, comfortable shelter high pay, abundance of churches, newspapers, libraries, charities, and a good education for everybody's child for nothing. He added, "society seems organized there for their benefit"—benefit of the bulk and mass of the people. Yes, it is conceded that we furnish the greater good to the greatest number; and so all we lack is a civilization.

Mr. Arnold's indicated civilization would seem to be restricted, by its narrow lines and difficult requirements, to a class—the top class—as in tropical countries snow is restricted to the mountain summits. And from what one may gather from his rather vague and unsure analysis of it, the snow metaphor would seem to fit it in more ways than one. The impression you get of it is, that it is peculiarly hard, and glistening, and bloodless, and unattainable. Now if our bastard were a civilization, it could fairly be figured—by Mr. Arnold's own concession—by the circulation of the blood, which nourishes and refreshes the whole body alike, delivering its rich streams of life and health impartially to the imperial brain and the meanest extremity.

"Advice to Youth"

Being told I would be expected to talk here, I inquired what sort of a talk I ought to make. They said it should be something suitable to youth—something didactic, instructive; or something in the nature of good advice. Very well; I have a few things in my mind which I have often longed to say for the instruction of the young; for it is in one's tender early years that such things will best take root and be most enduring and most valuable. First, then, I will say to you, my young friends—and say it beseechingly, urgingly—.

Always obey your parents, when they are present. This is the best policy in the long run; because if you don't they will make you. Most parents think they know better than you do; and you can generally make more by humoring that superstition than you can by acting on your own better judgement.

Be respectful to your superiors, if you have any; also to strangers, and sometimes to others. If a person offend you, and you are in doubt as to whether it was intentional or not, do not resort to extreme measures; simply watch your chance and hit him with a brick. That will be sufficient. If you shall find that he had not intended any offense, come out frankly and confess yourself in the wrong when you struck him; acknowledge it like a man, and say you didn't mean to. Yes, always avoid violence; in this age of charity and kindliness, the time has gone by for such things. Leave dynamite to the low and unrefined.

Go to bed early, get up early—this is wise. Some authorities say get up with one thing, some with another. But a lark is really the best thing to get up with. It gives you a splendid reputation with everybody to know that you get up with the lark; and if you get the right kind of a lark, and work at him right, you can easily train him to get up at half-past nine, every time—it is no trick at all.

Now as to the matter of lying. You want to be very careful about lying;

otherwise you are nearly sure to get caught. Once caught, you can never again be, in the eyes of the good and the pure, what you were before. Many a young person has injured himself permanently through a single clumsy and ill-finished lie, the result of carelessness born of incomplete training. Some authorities hold that the young ought not to lie at all. That, of course, is putting it rather stronger than necessary; still, while I cannot go quite so far as that, I do maintain, and I believe I am right, that the young ought to be temperate in the use of this great art until practice and experience shall give them that confidence, elegance and precision which alone can make the accomplishment graceful and profitable. Patience, diligence, painstaking attention to detail—these are the requirements; these, in time, will make the student perfect; upon these, and upon these only, may he rely as the sure foundation for future eminence. Think what tedious years of study, thought, practice, experience, went to the equipment of that peerless old master who was able to impose upon the whole world the lofty and sounding maxim that "Truth is mighty and will prevail"—the most majestic compound fracture of fact which any of women born has yet achieved. For the history of our race, and each individual's experience, are sown thick with evidences that a truth is not hard to kill, and that a lie well told is immortal. There in Boston is a monument to the man who discovered anesthesia; many people are aware, in these latter days, that man didn't discover it at all, but stole the discovery from another man. Is this truth mighty, and will it prevail? Ah, no, my hearers, the monument is made of hardy material, but the lie it tells will outlast it a million years. An awkward, feeble, leaky lie is a thing which you ought to make it your unceasing study to avoid; such a lie as that has no more real permanence than an average truth. Why, you might as well tell the truth at once and be done with it. A feeble, stupid, preposterous lie will not live two years—except it be a slander upon somebody. It is indestructible, then, of course, but that is no merit of yours. A final word; begin your practice of this gracious and beautiful art early—begin now. If I had begun earlier, I could have learned how.

Never handle firearms carelessly. The sorrow and suffering that have been caused through the innocent but heedless handling of firearms by the young! Only four days ago, right in the next farmhouse to the one where I am spending the summer, a mother, old and gray and sweet, one of the loveliest spirits in the land, was sitting at her work, when her young son crept in and got down an old, battered rusty gun which had not been touched for many years, and was supposed not to be loaded, and pointed it at her, laughing and threatening to shoot. In her fright she ran screaming and pleading toward the door on the other side of the room; but as she passed him he placed the gun almost against her very breast and pulled the trigger! He had supposed it was not loaded. And he was right: it wasn't. So there wasn't any harm done. It is the only case of the kind I ever heard of.

Therefore, just the same, don't you meddle with old unloaded firearms; they are the most deadly and unerring things that have ever been created by man. You don't have to take any pains at all, with them; you don't have to have a rest, you don't have to have any sights on the gun, you don't have to take aim, even. No, you just pick out a relative and bang away, and you are sure to get him. A youth who can't hit a cathedral at thirty yards with a Gatling gun in three-quarters of an hour, can take up an old empty musket and bag his mother every time, at a hundred. Think what Waterloo would have been if one of the armies had been boys armed with old rusty muskets supposed not to be loaded, and the other army had been composed of their female relations. The very thought of it makes me shudder.

There are many sorts of books; but good ones are the sort for the young to read. Remember that. They are a great, an inestimable, an unspeakable means of improvement. Therefore be careful in your selection, my young friends; be very careful, confine yourself exclusively to Robertson's *Sermons*, Baxter's *Saint's Rest, The Innocents Abroad,* and works of that kind.

But I have said enough. I hope you will treasure up the instructions which I have given you, and make them a guide to your feet and a light to your understanding. Build your character thoughtfully and painstakingly upon these precepts; and by and by, when you have got it built, you will be surprised and gratified to see how nicely and sharply it resembles everybody else's.

"Edmund Burke on Croker and Tammany"

Great Britain had a Tammany and a Croker a good while ago. This Tammany was in India, and it began its career with the spread of the English dominion after the battle of Plassey. Its first boss was Clive, a sufficiently crooked person sometimes, but straight as a yardstick when compared with the corkscrew crookedness of the second boss, Warren Hastings. That old-time Tammany was the India Company's government, and had its headquarters at Calcutta. Ostensibly it consisted of a Great Council of four persons, of whom one was the Governor General, Warren Hastings; really it consisted of one person—Warren Hastings—for by usurpation he concentrated all authority in himself, and governed the country like an autocrat.

Ostensibly the Court of Directors, sitting in London and representing the vast interests of the stockholders, was supreme in authority over the Calcutta Great Council, whose membership it appointed and removed at pleasure, whose policies it dictated, and to whom it conveyed its will in the form of sovereign commands; but whenever it suited Hastings, he ignored even that august body's authority and conducted the mighty affairs of the British empire in India to suit his own notions.

At his mercy was the daily bread of every official, every trader, every clerk, every civil servant, big and little, in the whole huge India Company's machine; and the man who hazarded his bread by any failure of subserviency to the Boss, lost it.

Now then, let the supreme masters of British India, the giant corporation of the India Company in London, stand for the voters of the City of New York; let the Great Council of Calcutta stand for Tammany; let the corrupt and money-grubbing great hive of serfs which served under the Indian Tammany's rod stand for the New York Tammany's serfs; let Warren Hastings stand for Richard Croker, and it seems to me that the parallel is exact and complete. And so, let us be properly pious and thank God and our good luck that we didn't invent Tammany!

No, it is English. We are always imitating England, sometimes to our advantage, oftenest the other way. And if we can't find something recent to imitate, we are willing to go back a hundred years to hunt for a chance.

The Calcutta Tammany—like our own Tammany—had but one principle, one policy, one moving spirit of action—avarice, money-lust. So that it got money it cared not a rap about the means and the methods. It was always ready to lie, forge, betray, steal, swindle, cheat, rob; and no promise, no engagement, no contract, no treaty made by its boss was worth the paper it was written on or the polluted breath that uttered it. Is the parallel still exact? It seems to me to be twins.

But there the parallel stops. Further it cannot go. Beyond that line our Boss and Warren Hastings are no longer kin. Beyond that line Warren Hastings stands alone in the history of modern Christendom. He stands alone, in a desolate and awful isolation; in a black solitude of perjury, treachery, heartlessness, shamelessness, and an indifference to guiltless suffering, pain and misery properly describable as fiendish. Beyond the stated line we will not insult Mr. Croker by bracketing his name with the unspeakable name of Warren Hastings.

The most of us know no Hastings but Macaulay's and there is good reason for that: when we try to read the impeachment charges against him we find we cannot endure the pain of the details. They burn, they blister, they wrench the heart; they drive us out of ourselves, they make us curse and swear; and we wonder why it took a dozen years to try that demon, when the mere reading of the first charge in the interminable list ought to have sent him to the scaffold before dark.

II.

However, that is a side issue. We are dealing with the parallel, now, and that reaches down only to the stated line drawn above.

Edmund Burke, regarded by many as the greatest orator of all times, conducted the case against Warren Hastings in that renowned trial which lasted years and which promises to keep its renown for centuries to come. I wish to quote some of the things he said. I wish to imagine him arraigning Mr. Croker and Tammany before the voters of New York City and pleading for the overthrow of that combined iniquity on the 5th of November. In the following passage, for "My Lords," read "Fellow Citizens." For "Kingdom" read "city". For "Parliamentary process" read "political campaign." For "two Houses" read "two parties":

My Lords, I must look upon it as an auspicious circumstance to this cause, in which the honor of the Kingdom is involved, that from the first commencement of our Parliamentary process to this the hour of solemn trial, not the smallest difference of opinion has arisen between the two Houses.

In the following, let "persons" stand for "Tammany." For "India" read "Tammany," For "Parliament" read "parties." For "nation" read "city." For "India" read "New York":

My Lords, there are persons who, looking rather upon what was to be found in our records and histories than what was to be expected from the public justice, had formed hopes consolatory to themselves and dishonorable to us. They flattered themselves that the corruptions of India would escape amidst the dissensions of Parliament. They are disappointed. They will be disappointed in all the rest of their expectations . . . What the greatest inquest of the nation has begun to its highest tribunal will accomplish. At length justice will be done to India.

In the following, for "Commons do" read "we who represent the Fusion ticket do." In the closing sentence of the paragraph, infer that Mr. Croker is more or less casually referred to:

My Lords, I must confess that amidst these encouraging prospects the Commons do not approach your bar without awe and anxiety. The magnitude of the interests which we have in charge will reconcile some degree of solicitude for the event with the undoubting confidence with which we repose ourselves upon your Lordship's justice. For we are men, my Lord, and men are so made, that it is not only the greatness of danger, but the value of the adventure, which measures the degree of our concern in every undertaking. I solemnly assure your Lordships that no standard is sufficient to estimate the value which the Commons set upon the event of the cause they now bring before you. My Lords, the business of this day is not the business of *this man*, it is not solely whether the prisoner at the bar be found innocent or guilty, but whether millions of mankind shall be made miserable or happy.

For "India" in the following, read "New York City." For "distant empire" read "city":

Your Lordships will see, in the progress of this cause, that there is not only a long, connected system of maxims and principles invented to justify them. Upon both of these you must judge. According to the judgement that you shall give upon the past transactions in India, inseparably connected as they are with the principles which support them, the whole character of your future government in that distant empire is to be unalterably decided. It will take its perpetual tenor, it will receive its final impression from the stamp of this very hour.

In the following, for "India" read "New York City." For "part of the British" read "city of the American." For "decided" read "affected." For "national" read "municipal." For "nation" read "city." For "Kingdom" read "community":

It is not only the interest of India, now the most considerable part of the British empire, which is concerned but the credit and honor of the British nation itself will be decided by this decision. We are to decide by this judgement whether the crimes of individuals are to be turned into the public guilt and national ignominy, or whether this nation will convert the very offenses which have thrown a transient shade upon its government into something that will reflect a permanent lustre upon the honor, justice, and humanity of this Kingdom.

In the following paragraph we will suppose that Mr. Croker's famous confession is referred to—his frank and blunt confession, under judicial examination, that his interest in the city government began and ended with the money to be gotten out of it. His words were, "*I am working for my pocket every time*":

In an early stage of the proceeding the criminal desired to be heard. He was heard; and he produced before the bar of the House that insolent and unbecoming paper which lies upon our table. It was deliberately given in his own hand, and signed with his own name.

In the following, for "Mr. Hastings" read "Mr. Croker":

We urge no crimes that were not crimes of forethought. We charge him with nothing that he did not commit upon deliberation—that he did not commit against advice, supplication, and remonstrance—that he did not commit against the direct command of lawful authority—that he did not commit after reproof and reprimand, the reproof and reprimand of those who were authorized by the laws to reprove and reprimand him. The crimes of Mr. Hastings are not only crimes in themselves, but aggravated by being crimes of contumacy. They were crimes, not against forms, but against those eternal laws of justice which are our rule and our birthright. His offenses are, not in formal, technical language, but in reality, in substance and effect, *high* crimes and high misdemeanors.

Here is something further that fits Mr. Croker's case:

When you consider the late enormous power of the prisoner—when you consider his criminal, indefatigable assiduity in the destruction of all recorded evidence—when you consider the influence he has over almost all living testimony—I believe your Lordships, and I believe the world, will be astonished that so much, so clear, so solid, and so conclusive evidence of all kinds has been obtained against him.

Here is some more about the two Tammanies, in the following strikingly faithful description of the New York situation of today. For "magistrates," in the second sentence, read "placement." For "Mr. Hastings," in the closing sentence of the extract, read "Mr. Croker":

There is nothing to be in propriety called people to *watch*, to inspect, to balance against the power of office. The power of office . . . is the sole power in the country: the consequence of which is, that, being a Kingdom of magistrates, what is commonly called the *esprit de corps* is strong in it. This spirit of the body predominates equally in all its parts; by which the members must consider themselves as having a common interest . . . No control upon them exists . . . Therefore, in a body so constituted, confederacy is easy, and has been general. Your Lordships are not to expect that should happen in such a body which has never happened in any body or corporation—that is, that they should, in any instance, be *a proper check and control upon themselves*. It is not in the nature of things . . . By means of this peculiar circumstance it has not been difficult for Mr. Hastings to embody abuse and to put himself at the head of a regular system of corruption.

We all realize that Tammany's fundamental principle is monopoly—monopoly of the office; monopoly of the public feed trough; monopoly of the blackmail derivable from protected gambling hells, protected prostitution houses, protected professional seducers of country girls for the New York prostitution market, and all that; monopoly all around, "in some sense of other." I know what I'm talking about, for I run a good deal with the police—and the clergy. It's the safest thing to do both here and for the hereafter. Here's a letter received by me yesterday, written by an Irish policeman, who signs his full name. Now here's what he says: "Sir, I'm a policeman and I saw an interview with you the other day. I must tell you the men are with Seth most to a man."

Now, that's good. He speaks out. It don't always do, however, for a man to speak out what he thinks. We can't all be independent. Wives and children take a good deal of independence from us. I've lost nearly all of mine. The letter continues: "I wish you success in your support of the Hon. Seth Low." That's even better. See, at the end he becomes respectful. That letter sounds good.

One of Burke's compact sentences indicates that the Indian Tammany's base rock is the same one that ours roosts upon:

The fundamental principle of the whole of the East India Company's system is monopoly, in some sense or other.

Here is another accurate piece of portraiture of Mr. Hastings-Croker:

He was fourteen years at the head of that service; and there is not an instance, no, not one single instance, in which he endeavored to detect corruption, or that he ever, in any one single instance, attempted to punish it; but the whole service, with that whole mass of enormity which he attributes to it, slept, as it were, at once under his terror and his protection: under the protection, if they did not dare to move against him; under terror, from his power to pluck out individuals and make a public example of them, when he thought fit. And therefore that service, under his guidance and influence, was, beyond even what its own nature disposed it to, a service of confederacy, a service of connivance, a service composed of various systems of guilt, of which Mr. Hastings was *the head and the protector*.

And now, at last, we find—and not without pain—that the prophetic eye of Edmund Burke has cast a sorrowing glance down the long procession of unborn years, and it falls with a dull thud upon Mr. Shepard. For "Englishmen" read "Tammany":

But now it is true, that after seeing the power and profits of these men—that there is neither power, profession, nor occupation to be had which a reputable person can exercise, except through that channel—men of higher castes, and born to better things, have thrown themselves into that disgraceful servitude, and have become menial servants to Englishmen, that they might. . . .

I have not quoted the whole of the passage; for its final clause contains reproach which Mr. Shepard has not earned. It would do him an injustice; and that is a thing which Edmund Burke never wittingly did to any man. If he were here and now he would know Mr. Shepard better than he was able to forecast him a century ago, and he would leave it out; therefore for the honor I bear the unsmirched great name of Edmund Burke I do him the justice to leave it out for him.

Now we come to the marvel of marvels—the immortal Irish orator's portrait of Richard Croker, as placed before us thinly disguised as Warren Hastings. He does not spring it upon you out of an atmosphereless vacancy, but leads you up to his great work with these notable words of introduction and preparation:

. . . So far as to the crimes. As to the criminal, we have chosen him on the same principle on which we selected the crimes. We have not chosen to bring before you a poor, puny, trembling delinquent, misled, perhaps, by those who ought to have taught him better, but who have afterwards oppressed him by their power, as they had first corrupted him by their example. Instances there have been many, wherein the punishment of minor offenses, in inferior person, has been made the means of screening crimes of a high order, and in men of high description. Our course is different. We have not brought before you an obscure offender, who, when his insignificance and weakness are weighed against the power of the prosecution, gives even to public justice something of the appearance of oppression. . . .

Then he flings Richard Croker upon the canvas. (For the first "India" read "Tammany"; for the second "India" read "New York City.") Consider this astonishing photograph—consider the amazing perfection of it: Richard Croker, detail by detail, in his moral personality, from topknot down to heeltap—and remember that the man who made it has been in his grave a hundred years! Croker is Tammany; Tammany is Croker; and experts of our own who know the combination to the marrow have not been able to depict it with an exacter brush:

WHAT BURKE SAID

No, my Lords, we have brought before you the first man of India, in rank, authority and station. We have brought before you the *chief of the tribe*, the head of the whole body of Eastern offenders, *a captain-general of iniquity*, under who *all the fraud, all the peculation, all the tyranny in India is embodied, disciplined, arrayed, and paid*. This is the person, my Lords, that we bring before you. We have brought before you such a person, that, if you strike at him with the firm and decided arm of justice, you will not have need of a great many more examples. *You strike at the whole corps if you strike at the head*.

WHAT OUR EXPERTS SAY

Letter to Croker from President of Anti-Croker League

In the meantime, we desire to emphasize the fact that it is entirely due to your political venality that corruption is rampant in our municipal government, and that the agencies of our civilizations are controlled by the depraved elements of society. Under your guidance and inspiration, Tammany Hall has been turned into a machine for stock jobbing purposes, and for furthering schemes in which you and your cronies are financially interested. Its energies are largely devoted to blackmailing corporations for the benefit of your private pockets. A gambler's syndicate, made up of your intimate political coadjutors, is running the Police Department, through its accredited agent, Chief Devery. It issues licenses to lawbreakers, and collects revenues from vice and crime. The income from moral degradation is regulated by certain Tammany leaders on a cash register basis. You are the chief beneficiary of this vile system, and with your share of the filthy spoils you manage to maintain a lordly estate in England.

The issue before the Lords was *Hastings and Hastingsism*; the only issue before New York in the imminent election is *Croker and Crokerism*. The two issues are the same, under differing names. If Edmund Burke were here he could change the names and make his speech again, and it would fit our circumstances exactly. Would he make it? We know by the heart of that great Irishman, and by his history, and by the noble hatred that was in him all form of wrong, dishonesty, chicane and oppression, that he would; and that he would beseech New York, with all the powers of his tongue and brain, and all the persuasions of his eloquence, to vote into obliteration and vacancy Mr. Croker and the infamies which he represents. And so we are privileged to imagine him here present and uttering again the righteous indignation which fell from his lips so long ago. And we know how he would close. We know that he would paraphrase his majestic impeachment of Warren Hastings, and say to the voters of New York:

"We know that we can commit safely the interests of this great metropolis into your hands. Therefore it is with confidence that, ordered by the people—

"I impeach Richard Croker of high crimes and misdemeanors.

"I impeach him in the name of the people, whose trust he has betrayed.

"I impeach him in the name of the people of America, whose national character he has dishonored.

"I impeach him in the name and by virtue of those eternal laws of justice which he has violated.

"I impeach him in the name of human nature itself, which he has cruelly outraged, injured, and oppressed, *in both sexes, in every age, rank, situation, and condition of life."*

"Our Guest" (Lord Mayor's Banquet)

My Lord Mayor, my Lord Bishop, and gentlemen: I want to thank you, my Lord Mayor, for the welcome you have given me tonight, and I thank these gentlemen for their hearty response in which they have received the toast; and I will thank—any other name? I only know him by "Tay Pay." I have another name—Langhorne—but it really doesn't belong to me.

Then you have a telegram from Professor Boyce, who says he still has a watch. That comes of having a fleeting reputation, I came to this country distinguished for honesty—and then somebody took that Ascot Cup just as I arrived, which has thrown a gloom over my whole stay here, and will provide sorrow and lamentations for my friends on the other side. And now I am held responsible for the regalia which has been stolen from Dublin Castle. What will become of my reputation if I do not get out of the country very soon? People say it is a curious coincidence that the Ascot Cup and the regalia from Dublin Castle should have been stolen during my stay, and so it is. I was going to Dublin. Fortunately for the rags of my reputation I could not get there.

And you say, what is this?—it is rumor. Nobody comes out and charges me with carrying away that robbery. It is mere human testimony, and it does not amount to testimony, it is merely rumor, circumstantial evidence, mere human speech, assertion, rumor and suspicion. But circumstantial evidence is the best evidence in the world. Once a month for five hundred years certain officers whose function it is go down the cellars in Dublin Castle, and there they find the safe in which the precious jewels are kept, and take them out one by one daily just to see that they are all right, and put them back in the safe. They have been doing this for five hundred years, and they have got so used to it that they did not shut up the safe. I should like to know whether that is a good safe and valuable safe. That is an important feature for me, because, with the reputation which I have got now, all the circumstantial evidence would point to the fact that if I took anything at all I would not merely have carried off the regalia, but the safe along with it. All this is testimony in my favor, and yet Professor Boyce is afraid to bring along his watch, which is probably only a Waterbury, and an old one at that.

Mr. O'Connor has furnished you information that enabled you to understand that I have been a jack-of-all-trades. That is quite true. He said a word about my father. He was a lawyer, but my father was entitled to more words than that. He was another of my kind. He was not just merely a lawyer, but in that little village on the banks of the Mississippi, when I was a boy, he was mayor of the town, the chief of police, the postmaster, the one policeman, and the sheriff who had to hang all the malefactors. In fact, he was the entire government—concentrated. Now, you can't pass by a man like that with just a word.

Mr. O'Connor spoke of my mother, too. Well, my brother and I were twins. He was born ten years before I was—a little discrepancy that never could be accounted for. It was the intention that brother of mine should be a lazy person. I know that perfectly well, but somehow or other it missed fire, and I was born that way instead. I have been lazy ever since, and indolent; while that brother, the twin—he was full of energy and the spirit of labor. Whatever he put his hand to he worked at it hard and faithfully, and the result was—the result was he could never make a living anyhow.

I can't help being frivolous tonight, because I have followed out my instructive and natural custom this afternoon by having a sleep and resting myself. Whenever I am rested and feeling good I can't help being frivolous. It is only when I am weary and worn-out and discouraged that the time comes for me to take a hold on great national questions and handle them. I wanted to talk real instructive wisdom tonight; but this rest has intervened, and put it all out of my mind.

I have been two or three weeks discussing cheap penny international postage with Mr. Henniker Heaton, and I have told him all I know about it. And now he knows nothing about it himself. I said I was born lazy, but I was born wise also; and the only time I ever lost a situation—the only time I was ever discharged from a post—was in San Francisco, more than forty years ago, when I was a reporter on the *Morning Call.* I was discharged just that once in my life, and the only thing they could bring against me was that I was incompetent, and incandescent, and inharmonious, and everything they could think of in three syllables; but mainly, I was lazy and inefficient. That was the only time anybody ever found fault with me for a thing like that. It was occurring all the time; in fact, it was monotonous, and it was no use picking out a thing like that.

According to Tay Pay, I have been a little of everything. This time I am an Ambassador. I like that position very well. I don't mind it as it has not a salary attached to it, because a salary limits your energy. It does mine, always. I would rather be free to do my ambassadorial work after my own fashion, and I intend to keep up this ambassadorial business right along. Whenever I find a chance of encouraging the good feeling between this old mother country and her eldest child over there, I intend to put in my word and keep up the ambassadorial work.

The University of Oxford, in making me a doctor, has added one more function to my numerous functions, and somebody asked me a rather pointed question—"Was it not rather a delicate thing to make you a Doctor of Literature? Are you competent to doctor your own a little?" That is all wrong. I have been doctoring my own literature. It is only now by the authority of Oxford that I propose to doctor other people's, and I hope you will see results. Why, I have always had an interest in literature outside my own concern. I have always been ready to give a helping hand to a rising young author.

I saved one poet in San Francisco forty years ago, and I don't forget it. I did a good turn to that poet. I was ready to doctor him or anybody else. Well, he wasn't much of a poet—a kind of poet good enough for the early days of the Pacific. He was not prosperous, and he was named Eddystone. We called him Eddystone Lighthouse. That was sarcasm. He was not a lighthouse. He was in trouble and I came to the young man's help. I was a reporter, but I was likely to lose the employment at any time, and I knew it would be such a good thing for me if I could do something rather extraordinary to keep ahead of the other papers.

Well, the young poet got discouraged. His poetry began to be a drug, he could not sell it, and by and by, when he could not give it away, his circumstances were desperate, and he came to me as a friend and wise adviser, and he proposed to commit suicide. I told him it was a good idea. It was a good idea in various ways. It would relieve him from writing poetry, and it would relieve the community from reading it, and it would give me a chance with my newspaper, I being the only other person present at the suicide—I would take care of that. He was a little sorry to see me so enthusiastic. I could not help that; my heart was in it.

We discussed methods, and I told him the most picturesque was the revolver to blow his brains out with. He did not like that idea very much, but I reconciled him to it. But we did not have any money to buy a revolver and we went round to the place with the three balls. There was a revolver there, just the right thing, but we could not borrow that revolver without furnishing some money. I told the gentleman that this was the only chance the young man had, but he was that kind of man that you could not persuade at all—a man who has no human sympathy, although it does not cost anything.

Then I suggested drowning to my friend. That would be a neat thing.

It could not be as fine for me as the other, but drowning was good enough when you could not get anything better. Se we went out to the seashore, and he did not like the looks of the water, and wanted me to try how it would go; but no, I was not in that line at all. Then a most curious thing—one of the strangest things, a thing you would never imagine at all—happened. From some ship, that had foundered perhaps a thousand miles away, there came an object of some interest at that moment. There were, in fact, two events gradually coming together. While this young man was brooding and contemplating suicide there was a life preserver floating in from that ship. A life preserver for a man who was about to commit suicide?

It looked ridiculous at first, but we took the life preserver to the pawnbroker and traded with him for the revolver. And then we made all the arrangements. But he didn't like to put the firearm to his forehead. I said, "It will be over in a minute," and this seemed to reassure him, for he bucked up and blew his brains out. People said it wasn't brains; but it was. There was not much of it; but is was real grey matter, which is supposed to constitute intelligence so far as it can. Well, that was the making of that boy. Why, when he got well, all obstructions were gone! And I have thought many times since that if poets when they get discouraged would blow their brains out, they could write very much better when they got well.

I landed in this town of Liverpool thirty years ago—the first time I ever put my foot on English soil—and I had an adventure. As a matter of fact, Liverpool is connected with one of two adventures of a very pleasant sort. I went to the outside edge of town, and I saw the scenery—the blocked-up windows to escape the window tax, and various other exciting things—and finally, I took a cab and drove around. The man was a very good-natured, pleasant, middle-aged Scotchman, and he asked where he should drive me to. I said anywhere just around for an hour or two hours. He drove me a little way, and then stopped and asked me again. Well, I wanted to think—I was full of some great project—and finally, when this had occurred several more times, in desperation I said, "Oh, take me to Balmoral."

I did not say a word, and I did not pay any attention to where he was going. I wanted to think. I did not know where I was. I was away somewhere in the country, and I hailed him and asked him where he was going, and he said, "On the way to Balmoral." So he was. I got him to turn round and get back to Liverpool if he could, to catch a train for London, if possible. When we got back I asked him what I had to pay, and he said—well, it was equivalent to four hundred dollars. I asked him if he was in earnest, and he said he was, as outside the city he could charge any reasonable price. He said that Balmoral was four hundred miles away, and it would be four hundred dollars.

It seemed a sorry and embarrassing situation. I proposed to go before the rulers of the city or his Majesty or something of that sort to lay the case and he did. I said he had made a mistake, and the authorities said he had a right to charge anything reasonable. It seemed a large sum he had charged, and they said it was not the cabman's fault—it was four hundred miles to Balmoral and four shillings a mile was not unreasonable, especially as he would have to come back at his own expense. Well, the man acted very handsomely; he compromised for twelve dollars. Though stupid tradition says that Scotchmen did not profess a sense of humor, I say that man has a sense of humor.

What was Tay Pay's early statement that requires refutation? [Mr. O'Connor: "I said that you had been a financier."] I was, but I am not now; I didn't succeed in it. He also mentioned another matter, and he paid me the compliment to mention that at the time when I was bankrupt, heavily in debt, I paid every dollar. This is often mentioned—very pleasing to me to hear—and I feel that I ought to get on my feet and tell you all about it—how my business man, my longheaded commercial friend said, "In this bankruptcy business you pay thirty cents to the dollar and you go free." Now, a man can easily be persuaded to go outside the strict moral line, but it is not so with a woman and a wife. My wife said, "No, you shall pay a hundred cents to the dollar and I will go with you all the way." And she kept her word. Let us give credit where credit is due, and it is more due her than to me.

I don't think I will say anything about the relations of amity existing between our two countries. It is not necessary, it seems to me. The ties between the two nations are so strong that I do not think we need trouble ourselves about them being broken. Anyhow, I am quite sure that in my time, and in yours, my Lord Mayor, those ties will hold good, and please God, they always will. English blood is in our veins, we have a common language, a common religion, a common system of morals, and great commercial interests to hold us together.

Home is dear to us all, and I am now departing for mine on the other side of the ocean. Oxford has conferred upon me the loftiest honor that has ever fallen to my fortune, the one I should have chosen as outranking any and all others and more precious to me than any and all others within the gift of men and states to bestow upon me. And I have had, in the four weeks that I have been here, another lofty honor: a continuous honor, an honor which has known no interruption in all these twenty-six days, and a most moving and pulse-stirring honor: the hearty hand grip and the cordial welcome which does not descend from the pale grey matter of the brain, but comes up with the red blood out of the heart! It makes me proud, and it makes me humble. Many and many a year ago I read an anecdote in Dana's book, *Two Years Before the Mast*. A frivolous little self-important captain of a coasting sloop in the dried apple and kitchen furniture trade was always hailing every vessel that came in sight, just to hear himself talk, and air his small grandeurs. One day a majestic Indiaman came plowing by, with course on course of canvas towering into the sky, her decks and years swarming with sailors; with macaws and monkeys and all manner of strange and romantic creatures populating her rigging; and thereto her freightage of precious spices lading the breeze with gracious and mysterious odors of the Orient. Of course, the little coaster captain hopped into the shrouds and squeaked out a hail: "Ship ahoy! what ship is that, and whence and whither?" In a deep and thunderous bass came the answer back through a speaking trumpet: "The *Begum of Bengal*, a hundred and twenty-three days out from Canton—homeward bound! What ship is that?" The little captain's vanity was all crushed out of him, and most humbly he squeaked back: "Only the *Mary Ann*—fourteen hours out from Boston, bound for Kittery Point with —with nothing to speak of!" The eloquent word "only" expressed the deeps of his stricken humbleness.

And what is my own case? During perhaps one hour in the twenty-four—not more than that—I stop and reflect. Then I am humble, then I am properly meek, and for that little time I am "only the *Mary Ann*," fourteen hours out, and cargoed with vegetables and tinware; but all the other twenty-three my vain self-satisfaction rides high and I am the stately Indiaman, plowing the great seas under a cloud of sail, and laden with a rich freightage of the kindest words that were ever spoken to a wandering alien, I think; my twenty-six crowded and fortunate days seem multiplied by five, and I am the *Begum of Bengal*, a hundred and twenty-three days out from Canton—homeward bound!

"Dinner Speech" (Seventieth Birthday)

Well, if I made that joke, it is the best one I ever made, and it is in the prettiest language, too. I never can get quite to that height. But I appreciate that joke, and I shall remember it—and I shall use it when occasion requires.

I have had a great many birthdays in my time. I remember the first one very well, and I always think of it with indignation; everything was so crude, unesthetic, primeval. Nothing like this at all. No proper appreciative preparation made; nothing really ready. Now, for a person born with high and delicate instincts—why, even the cradle wasn't whitewashed—nothing ready at all. I hadn't any hair, I hadn't any teeth, I hadn't any clothes. I had to go to my first banquet just like that. Well, everybody came swarming in. It was the merest little bit of a village—hardly that, just a little hamlet, in the backwoods of Missouri, where nothing ever happened, and the people were all interested, and they all came; they looked me over to see if there was anything fresh in my line. Why, nothing ever happened in that village—I why, I was the only thing that had really happened there for months and months and months; and although I say it myself that shouldn't, I came the nearest to being a real event that had happened in that village in more than two years. Well, those people came, they came with that curiosity which is so provincial, with that frankness which also is so provincial, and they examined me all around and gave their opinion. Nobody asked them, and I shouldn't have minded if anybody had paid me a compliment, but nobody did. Their opinions were all just green with prejudice, and I feel those opinions to this day. Well, I stood that as long as—well, you know I was born courteous, and I stood it to the limit. I stood it an hour, and then the worm turned. I was the worm; it was my turn to turn, and I turned. I knew very well the strength of my position; I knew that I was the only spotlessly pure and innocent person in that whole town, and I came out and said so. And they could not say a word. It was so true. They blushed, they were embarrassed. Well, that was the first after-dinner speech I ever made. I think it was after dinner.

It's a long stretch between that first birthday speech and this one. That was my cradle song, and this is my swan song. I suppose, I am used to swan songs; I have sung them several times.

This is my seventieth birthday, and I wonder if you all rise to the size of that proposition, realizing all the significance of that phrase, seventieth birthday.

The seventieth birthday! It is the time of life when you arrive at a new and awful dignity; when you may throw aside the decent reserves which have oppressed you for a generation and stand unafraid and unabashed upon your seven-terraced summit and look down and teach—unrebuked. You can tell the world know you got there. It is what they all do. You shall never get tired of telling by what delicate arts and deep moralities you climbed up to that great place. You will explain the process and dwell on the particulars with senile rapture. I have been anxious to explain my own system this long item, and now at last I have the right.

I have achieved my seventy years in the usual way: by sticking strictly to a scheme of life which would kill anybody else. It sounds like an exaggeration, but that is really the common rule for attaining to old age. When we examine the program of any of these garrulous old people we always find that the habits which have preserved them would have decayed us: that the way of life which enabled them to live upon the property of their heirs so long, as Mr. Choate says, would have put us out of commission ahead of time. I will offer here, as a sound maxim, this: that we can't reach old age by another man's road.

I will now teach, offering my way of life to whomsoever desires to commit suicide by the scheme which has enabled me to beat the doctor and the hangman for seventy years. Some of the details may sound untrue, but they are not. I am not here to deceive; I am here to teach.

We have no permanent habits until we are forty. Then they begin to harden, presently they petrify, then business begins. Since forty I have been regular about going to bed and getting up—and that is one of the main things. I have made it a rule to go to bed when there wasn't anybody left to sit up with; and I have made a rule to get up when I had to. This has resulted in an unswerving regularity of irregularity. It has saved me sound, but it would injure another person.

In the matter of diet—which is another main thing—I have been persistently strict in sticking to the things which didn't agree with me until one of the other of us got the best of it. Until lately I got the best of it myself. But last spring I stopped frolicking with mince pie after midnight; up to then I and always believed it wasn't loaded. For thirty years I have taken coffee and bread at eight in the morning, and no bite nor sup until seven-thirty in the evening. Eleven hours. That is all right for me, and is wholesome, because I have never had a headache in my life, but headachy people would not reach seventy comfortably by that road, and they would be foolish to try it. And I wish to urge upon you this—which I think is wisdom—that if you find you can't make seventy by any but an uncomfortable road, don't you go. When they take off the Pullman and retire you to the rancid smoker, put on your things, count your cheeks, and get out at the first way station where there's a cemetery.

I have made it a rule never to smoke more than one cigar at a time. I have no other restriction as regards smoking. I do not know just when I began to smoke, I only know that it was in my father's lifetime, and that I was discreet. He passed form this life early in 1847, when I was a shade past eleven; ever since then I have smoked publicly. As an example to others, and not that I care for moderation myself, it has always been my rule never to smoke when asleep, and never to refrain when awake. It is a good rule, I mean for me; but some of you know quite well that it wouldn't answer for everybody that's trying to get to be seventy.

I smoke in bed until I have to go to sleep; I wake up in the night, sometimes once, sometimes twice, sometimes three times, and I never waste any of these opportunities to smoke. This habit is so old and dear and precious to me that I would feel as you, sir, would feel if you should lose the only moral you've got—meaning the chairman—if you've got one; I am making no chafes. I will grand, here, that I have stopped smoking now and then, for a few months at a time, but it was not on principal, it was only to show off; it was to pulverize those critics who said I was a slave to my habits and couldn't break my bonds. Today it is all of sixty years since I began to smoke the limit. I have never bought cigars with life belts around them. I early found that those were too expensive for me. I have always bought cheap cigars—reasonably cheap, at any rate. Sixty years ago they cost me four dollars a barrel, but my taste has improved, latterly, and I pay seven now. Six or seven. Seven, I think. Yes it's seven. But that includes the barrel. I often have smoking parties at my house; but the people that come have always just taken the pledge. I wonder why that is?

As for drinking, I have no rule about that. When the others drink I like to help; otherwise I remain dry, by habit and preference. This dryness does not hurt me, but it could easily hurt you, because you are different. You let it alone.

Since I was seven years old I have seldom taken a dose of medicine, and have still seldomer needed one. But up to seven I lived exclusively on allopathic medicines. Not that I needed them, for I don't think I did; it was for economy; my father took a drug store for a debt, and it made cod liver oil cheaper than other breakfast foods. We had nine barrels of it, and it lasted me seven years. Then I was weaned. The rest of the family had to get along with rhubarb and ipecac and such things, because I was the pet. I was the first Standard Oil Trust. I had it all. By the time the drug store was exhausted my health was established and there has never been much the matter with me since. But you know very well it would be foolish for the average child to start for seventy on that basis. It happened to be just the thing for me, but that was merely an accident; it couldn't happen again in a century.

I have never taken any exercise, except sleeping and resting, and I never intend to take any. Exercise is loathsome. And it cannot be any benefit when you are tired; and I was always tired. But let another person try my way, and see where he will come out.

I desire now to repeat and emphasize that maxim: We can't reach old age by another man's road. My habits protect my life but they would assassinate you.

I have lived a severely moral life. But it would be a mistake for other people to try that, or for me to recommend it. Very few would succeed: you have to have a perfectly colossal stock of morals; and you can't get them on a margin; you have to have the whole thing, and put them in your box. Morals are an acquirement—like music, like a foreign language, like piety, poker, paralysis—no man is born with them. I wasn't myself. I started poor. I hadn't a single moral. There is hardly a man in this house that is poorer than I was then. Yes, I started like that—the world before me, not a moral in the slot. Not even an insurance moral. I can remember the first one I ever got. I can remember the landscape, the weather, the—I can remember how everything looked. It was an old moral, an old secondhand moral, all out of repair, and didn't fit, anyway. But if you are careful with a thing like that, and keep it in a dry place, and save it for processions, and chautauquas, and World's Fairs, and so on, and disinfect it now and then, and give it a fresh coat of whitewash once in a while, you will be surprised to see how well she will last and how long she will keep sweet, or at least inoffensive. When I got that mouldy old moral, she had stopped growing, because she hadn't any exercise; but I worked her hard. I worked her Sundays and all. Under this cultivation she waxed in might and stature beyond belief, and served me well and was my pride and joy for sixty-three years; then she got to associating with insurance presidents, and lost flesh and character, and was a sorrow to look at and no longer competent for business. She was a great loss to me. Yet not all loss. I sold her—ah, pathetic skeleton, as she was—I sold her to Leopold, the pirate King of Belgium; he sold her to our Metropolitan Museum, and it was very glad to get her, for, without a rag on, she stands fifty-seven feet long and sixteen feet high, and they think she's a brontosaur. Well, she looks it. They believe it will take nineteen geological periods to breed her match.

Morals are of inestimable value, for every man is born crammed with sin microbes, and the only thing that can extirpate these sin microbes is morals. Now, you take a sterilized Christian—I mean, you take *the* sterilized Christian, for there's only one. Dear sir, I wish you wouldn't look at me like that.

Threescore years and ten!

It is the Scriptural statute of limitations. After that, you owe no active duties; for you the strenuous life is over. You are a time-expired man, to use Kipling's military phrase. You have served your term, well or less well, and you are mustered out. You are become an honorary member of the republic, you are emancipated, compulsions are not for you, nor any bugle call but "lights out." You pay the timeworn duty bills if you choose, or decline if you prefer—and without prejudice—for they are not legally collectible.

The previous engagement plea, which in forty years has cost you so many twinges, you can lay aside forever, on this side of the grave you will never need it again. If you shrink at thought of night, and winter, and the late homecoming from the banquet and the lights and the laughter through the deserted streets—a desolation which would not remind you now, as for a generation it did, that your friends are sleeping, and you must creep in a-tiptoe and not disturb them, but would only remind you that you need not tiptoe, you can never disturb them more—if you shrink at thought of these things, you need only reply. "Your invitation honors me, and pleases me because you still keep me in your remembrance, but I am seventy; seventy, and would nestle in the chimney corner, and smoke my pipe, and read my book, and take my rest, wishing you well in all affection, and that when you in your turn shall arrive at pier No. 70 you may step aboard your waiting ship with a reconciled spirit, and lay your course toward the sinking sun with a contented heart."

Chronology of Significant Speaking Events

The purpose of this chronology is to give the reader an overview of Mark Twain's public speaking career. Twain spoke hundreds of times to thousands of listeners on sundry occasions. He spoke for money, when necessary, and for charity, with preference; he spoke against corruption and for human rights. His motive remained constant—to teach democratic values.

DATE	PLACE	SPEECH
1866		
October 2	Maguire's Opera House, San Francisco	"Sandwich Islands"
October 11-November 27	California and Nevada	"Sandwich Islands" (Lecture Tour-16 engagements)
December 10	Congress Hall, San Francisco	"Sandwich Islands"
1867		
March 25-April 9	Midwest lecture tour	"Sandwich Islands"

DATE	PLACE	SPEECH
May 6	Cooper Union, New York City	"Sandwich Islands"
May 10	Athenaeum, Brooklyn	"Sandwich Islands"
May 15	Irving Hall, New York City	"Sandwich Islands"
August 25	Yalta, Russia (*Quaker City* tour)	"Address to the Czar"
1868		
January 9	Metzerott Hall, Washington, D.C.	"The Frozen Truth" (*Quaker City* experience)
January 11	Newspaper Correspondents Dinner, Washington D.C.	"Woman—The Pride of Any Profession and the Jewel of Ours"
April 14-15	Platt's Hall, San Francisco	"Pilgrim Life" (*Quaker City* experience)
April 17-30	California and Nevada (Lecture Tour-9 engagements)	"Pilgrim Life"
July 2	Mercantile Library, San Francisco	"Venice" (*Quaker City* experience)

DATE	PLACE	SPEECH
November 17-March 3, 1869	Eastern Lecture Tour (for Boston Lyceum-42 engagements)	"The American Vandal Abroad"
1869		
November 1-January 21, 1870	Lecture Tour (45 engagements)	"Our Fellow Savages of the Sandwich Islands"
1870		
January 31	Benefit for Father Hawley, Hartford	"Sandwich Islands"
1871		
October 16-February 6, 1872	Lecture Tour (77 engagements)	"Uncommonplace Characters," "Artemis Ward," "Roughing It"
1872		
September 22	Savage Club, London	Dinner Speech
1873		
January 31	Benefit for Father Hawley, Hartford	"Sandwich Islands"
February 5	Steinway Hall, New York City	"Sandwich Islands"

DATE	PLACE	SPEECH
February 7	Brooklyn	"Sandwich Islands"
February 10	Steinway Hall, New York City	"Sandwich Islands"
October 13-18	Queen's Concert Rooms, London	"Sandwich Islands"
October 20, 25	Liverpool Institute, Liverpool	"Sandwich Islands"
November (?)	Scottish Corporation, London	"The Ladies"
December 1-7	Queen's Concert Rooms, London	"Sandwich Islands"
December 8-19	Queen's Concert Rooms, London	"Roughing It"
1874		
January 8	Leicester	"Roughing It"
January 9, 10	Liverpool	"Roughing It"
September 16	Park Theatre, New York City (At the opening of Twain's play *The Gilded Age*)	Curtain Speech
October 12	Insurance Men's Dinner, Hartford	Dinner Speech

DATE	PLACE	SPEECH
1875		
March 5	For Father Hawley, Hartford	"Roughing It"
1881		
June 8	Army of the Potomac Banquet, Hartford	"The Benefit of Judicious Training"
December 22	New England Society, Philadelphia	"Plymouth Rock and the Pilgrims"
1882		
April 15	Saturday Morning Club, Boston	"Advice to Youth"
1883		
May 23	Royal Literary and Scientific Society Dinner, Ottawa	"On Adam"
1884		
October (?)	Mugwump Rally, Hartford	"Turncoats"
October 20	Mugwump Rally, Hartford	Remarks as Chairman
November 28-February 28, 1885	Reading Tour with Cable (103 engagements)	Passages from his books and *Huckleberry Finn* manuscript

DATE	PLACE	SPEECH
1885		
March 31	Hutton Dinner, New York City	"On Speech-Making Reform"
1887		
April 27	Army and Navy Club, Hartford	Dinner Speech (A patriotic attack on foreign critics)
December 20	Congregationalist Club, Boston	"Post-Prandial Oratory"
1890		
January 20	Broadway Theatre, New York City (At the opening of Twain's play *The Prince and the Pauper)*	Curtain Speech
April 27	Max O'Rell Dinner, Boston	"On Foreign Critics"
1891		
May 22	Herald Square Theatre, New York City (At the opening of Twain's play *Pudd'nhead Wilson*)	Curtain Speech

DATE	PLACE	SPEECH
July 15, **1895**-July **1896**	World Speaking Tour: United States, Canada, Australia, New Zealand, India, Ceylon, Mauritius, South Africa (about 140 engagements)	Morals Lecture

From **1897** through half of **1900**,Twain spoke abroad—London,Vienna, Budapest, and back to London.

1900

November 23	Public Education Association, New York City	Remarks (anti-imperialism)
December 12	Waldorf-Astoria, New York City	"Introducing Winston S. Churchill" (anti-imperialism)

1901

January 4	City Club, New York City	"Municipal Corruption"
March 16	Male Teachers Association	"Training That Pays" (teach children democratic ideals)
October 17	Acorns, New York City	"Edmund Burke on Croker and Tammany"

DATE	PLACE	SPEECH
1902		
November 28	Sixty-Seventh Birthday Dinner, New York City	Dinner Speech
1905		
December 5	Seventieth Birthday, New York City	Dinner Speech
1907		
July 4	American Society, London	"The Day We Celebrate"
July 6	Savage Club, London	Dinner Speech
July 10	Lord Mayor's Dinner, Liverpool	"Our Guest"
1908		
May 25	British Schools and Universities Club, New York City	"Queen Victoria—An American Tribute"
June 9	Misses Tewksbury's School, Baltimore	Remarks (Twain's last public speech—on morals)

Bibliographic Essay

This bibliography is divided into five sections for the reader's convenience. The first discusses the Mark Twain collections found in various libraries. The second section deals with those sources which address Twain's speeches exclusively. The section is divided into three parts—the volumes that are collections of Twain's speeches, the works that offer a rhetorical analysis of his performances, and other critical works that focus on his speaking career. The third section reviews select biographical sources that offer insight into the speaker himself and his feelings about public speaking. The fourth section presents sources that aid in understanding the rhetorical situations that Twain addressed. The fifth section lists general sources which serve to increase the reader's understanding of public address and rhetorical criticism. The purpose of this essay is to provide the reader with a comprehensive guide to the available literature that supports the critical study of Mark Twain's public speaking career.

RESEARCH COLLECTIONS

The most thorough collection on Mark Twain, known as the Mark Twain Papers, is located at the Bancroft Library of the University of California at Berkeley. The collection includes copies of some fifty notebooks kept by the author; approximately 28,000 letters written by and to Twain and his family members; and some 600 literary manuscripts. There are also Twain's working notes, manuscript drafts, printers' proofs; first editions of his published works; and family photographs. Mark Twain's personal library collection, including his books on oratory and rhetoric, can be found on the shelves: *Select*

Orations of Cicero, *Letters on Rhetorik* by J.L. Blake, *Essentials of Elocution and Oratory* by V.A. Pinkley, *The Ghosts and Other Lectures* by Robert Green Ingersoll, *Yale Lectures on Preaching and Other Writings*, edited by Richard E. Burton, and *The Technique of Speech: A Guide to the Study of Diction According to the Principles of Resonance*. (For further information, see Alan Gribben, *Mark Twain's Library: A Reconstruction*, 2 vols. Boston: G. K. Hall & Company, 1980.) In addition, the collection contains his business documents, interviews, and a working library of secondary sources.

The Mark Twain Project, an editorial and publishing program, is currently working on a comprehensive scholarly edition of all Twain's private papers and published works. So far, nineteen volumes of the proposed 70-volume edition has been published. Of particular interest are the following: Anderson, Frederick, et al., eds., *Mark Twain's Notebooks and Journals* 3 vols. (Berkeley: University of California Press, 1975-79); Branch, Edgar Marquess, Michael B. Frank, and Kenneth M. Sanderson, eds., *Mark Twain's Letters*, 1 [1853-1866], (Berkeley: University of California Press, 1988); and Smith, Harriet Elinor, Richard Bucci, and Lin Salamo, eds., *Mark Twain's Letters*, 2 [1867-1868], (Berkeley: University of California Press, 1990).

Other library collections tend to offer little specific information about Twain's speaking career. The Henry W. and Albert A. Berg Collection at the New York Public Library includes first edition copies of *Mark Twain's Autobiography, Mark Twain's Letters* (1917), and *Mark Twain's Speeches* (1910, 1923). The collection also contains first edition copies and/or manuscripts of four speeches: "Edmund Burke on Croker and Tammany," "Taxes and Morals," "The Babies," and "The Ladies." "The Ladies" manuscript is written by both Clemens and his wife, Olivia Langdon Clemens. At the Vassar College Library, Mark Twain papers are part of the Jean Webster McKinney Family Papers collection. There is Twain's earliest surviving notebook and many of his letters. Much of Twain's papers deal with his business adventures. (Jean Webster McKinney's father was Charles Webster, Twain's nephew and business manager.) However, the papers of Isabel Van Kleek Lyon, Twain's personal secretary from 1903-1909, offer the researcher an intimate glimpse into Twain's later years. The Lyons papers contain written records, such as diaries and daybooks, and memorabilia, including family photographs, of these years.

At the Clifton Waller Barrett Library of American Literature at the University of Virginia is the Mark Twain Collection, which contains books and manuscripts. Only sixteen sources appear to deal with Twain's speeches.

The Mark Twain Collection at the Houghton Library of Harvard University contains little dealing with Twain's speaking career—some letters to James Redpath about lecturing, a letter to Emerson (1877), and a collection of printed material about Twain's seventieth birthday.

Consulting Thomas Asa Tenney's, *Mark Twain: A Reference Guide* (Boston, Mass.: G.K. Hall & Co., 1977) and his "Seventh Annual Supplement" (*American Literary Realism* 16 [1983], 163-222) is a recommended way to begin research on Mark Twain. This volume, with annual supplements published in *American Literary Realism*, present an up-to-date, chronologically organized, annotated bibliography of writings about Twain. Another worthwhile bibliographic source is Robert Rodney's *Mark Twain International: A Bibliography and Interpretation of His World-Wide Popularity* (Westport, Conn.: Greenwood Press, 1982). Because it is difficult, if not impossible, to separate Twain the author from Twain the public speaker, bibliographic essays that focus on his writings can offer valuable information to the student of Twain's oratory. Two good examples are Louis J. Budd's article "Mark Twain," (*American Literary Scholarship* [1983], 97-107) and Alan Gribben's "Removing Mark Twain's Mask: A Decade of Criticism and Scholarship" (*ESQ: A Journal of the American Renaissance* 26 [1980], 149-171).

SOURCES THAT ARE PRIMARILY CONCERNED WITH TWAIN'S ORATORY

Aside from this series, *American Orators Before 1900: Critical Studies and Sources*, edited by Bernard K. Duffy and Halford R. Ryan (Westport, Conn.: Greenwood Press, 1987), is the only anthology of American orators that includes Mark Twain. It contains a brief overview of Twain's background with an abbreviated bibliography, written by Richard J. Calhoun. What is most significant about this essay is the author's awareness of the need to recognize Twain's rhetorical skills.

Speech Collections

Three collections of Twain's speeches have been published. Clemens, Samuel L., *Mark Twain's Speeches* with an Introduction by William Dean Howells, was first compiled by F. A. Nast (New York: Harper & Brothers Publishers, 1910). *Mark Twain's Speeches*, with an Introduction by Albert Bigelow Paine and an Appreciation by William Dean Howells, was reissued, with some changes in the selection of speeches, by the same publisher in 1923. Paine's "Introduction" and Howell's "Appreciation" provide an intimate appraisal of Twain's speaking talent. *Mark Twain Speaking*, edited by Paul Fatout (Iowa City: University of Iowa Press, 1976) is the most thorough anthology. There are more speeches included, and each speech is prefaced with details about the occasion and followed by an explanation of terms and names. Fatout's volume also includes a very extensive annotated chronology.

Rhetorical Analyses

Three sources regard Twain's platform performances from a rhetorical perspective. Frederick J. Antczak's *Thought and Character: The Rhetoric of Democratic Education* (Ames: The Iowa State University Press, 1985) examines the spread of democratic ideals in the nineteenth century. He credits the platforms of public speech, in particular, the rhetoric of Twain, along with Ralph Waldo Emerson and William James. Two journal articles, written by Marlene Boyd Vallin, deal exclusively with Twain's performances: "Mark Twain, Platform Artist: A Nineteenth-Century Preview of Twentieth-Century Performance Theory," (*Text and Performance Quarterly* 9 [October 1989], 322-333) and "'Manner Is Everything': The Secret to Mark Twain's Performing Success," (*Journal of Popular Culture* 24 [Fall 1990], 81-90). The former posits that Twain's interpretation of the speech act was prescient. The article demonstrates this contention by comparing Twain's notions with the those formulated by modern rhetorical theorists James Winans and Charles Woolbert. The second article by Vallin demonstrates that Twain's platform success was the result of his extraordinary sense of audience.

Descriptive/Critical Accounts

Because Mark Twain was such an inveterate notetaker and letter writer, information about his public speaking career can be obtained from his own writings. In addition to the volumes produced by the Mark Twain Project and published by the University of California Press, which have collated Twain's notebooks and letters, there are other sources. Particularly noteworthy is the two-volume *Mark Twain's Autobiography*, edited and introduced by Albert Bigelow Paine (New York and London: Harper & Brothers Publishers, 1924). In this rambling, rather distorted dictation (According to Paine, the result of a "capricious memory" and "his vivid imagination" [p. x]), Twain comments extensively about his membership in the Boston Lyceum, his presentation of "The Babies" at the Thirteenth Reunion Banquet of the Army of the Tennessee, the "Sandwich Islands Lecture," and his Seventieth Birthday Speech. Charles Neider presents a chronologically organized version of this work, with the addition of material left by Twain after his death, in *The Autobiography of Mark Twain: Including Chapters Now Published for the First Time* (New York: Harper & Row, Publishers, 1959).

Other comments about his speaking career can be found in *Mark Twain's*

Notebook, prepared for publication with comments by Albert Bigelow Paine (New York and London: Harper & Brothers, 1935). This book contains a selection of materials from Mark Twain's unpublished notebooks from river pilot days to 1906. Also, the following collections of Twain's letters contain further comments: Clemens, Samuel, *Mark Twain's Letters*, arranged with comment by Albert Bigelow Paine (New York and London: Harper & Brothers Publishers, 1917) 2 vols.; Smith, Henry Nash, and William M. Gibson, eds., *Mark Twain-Howells Letters: The Correspondence of Samuel L. Clemens and William D. Howells, 1872-1910* (Cambridge, Mass.: The Belknap Press of Harvard University Press, 1960); Wecter, Dixon, ed., *Mark Twain to Mrs. Fairbanks* (San Marino, Cal.: Huntington Library, 1949); and Wecter, Dixon, ed., *The Love Letters of Mark Twain* (New York: Harper & Brothers, 1949).

There are other sources with Twain's comments about the communication process. *Mark Twain in Eruption: Hitherto Unpublished Pages about Men and Events by Mark Twain* (New York: Harpers and Brothers Publishers, 1922) contains Twain's notions on how to speak and read effectively in public. Also included are his adaptation for performance of "His Grandfather's Old Ram" and a complete chapter about his last visit to England. Twain's *Literary Essays* (New York: Harper and Brothers, 1918) has the instructional "How to Tell a Story," which describes Twain's concept of the humorous story. Paul Fatout's collection of Twain's comments, *Mark Twain Speaks for Himself* (West Lafayette, Indiana: Purdue University Press, 1978), come from those made in newspaper and magazine articles. Organized chronologically, this work provides insight into the development of Twain's ethos. Louis J. Budd's article "Mark Twain Talks Mostly about Humor and Humorists," (*Studies in American Humor* I [April 1974], 4-19) contains Twain's statements on humor as found in his essay "How to Tell a Story" and in various newspaper interviews. The actor Hal Holbrook had the script as well as the notes for the planning and preparation of his one-man show *Mark Twain Tonight!* published in 1959: *Mark Twain Tonight! An Actor's Portrait* (New York: Ives Washburn, Inc.).

For an in-depth review of Twain's experience on the lecture circuit, there are two books devoted exclusively to the topic: Fatout, Paul, *Mark Twain on the Lecture Circuit* (Carbondale: Southern Illinois University Press, 1960) and Lorch, Fred W., *The Trouble Begins at Eight* (Ames, Iowa: Iowa State University Press, 1968). Both volumes credit these platform experiences for the meteoric rise of Twain's popularity. Lorch's book is especially helpful for those interested in Twain's audiences and his platform techniques. Lorch's work also contains the texts of his five major lectures.

Fred W. Lorch also wrote journal articles that include the text of specific lectures and some background material: "Mark Twain's Sandwich Island

Lecture at St. Louis" (*American Literature* XVIII [1946-1947], 299-307), "Mark Twain's Lecture from *Roughing It*" (*American Literature* 17 [1950-1951], 290-307); "Mark Twain's 'Morals' Lecture during the American Phrase of His World Tour in 1895-1896" (*American Literature* 26 [March 1954], 52-66); "Mark Twain's Lecture Tour of 1868-1869: 'The American Vandal Abroad'" (*American Literature* XXVI [January 1955], 515-527); and "Mark Twain's Public Lectures in England in 1873 (*American Literature* XXIX [November 1957], 297-304).

There are a number of interesting contemporary appraisals of Twain's lecturing: for example, "Mark Twain on the Lecture Platform," an article written by Will M. Clemens for *Ainslee's Magazine* (6 [August 1900], 32) contains extracts from some of Twain's letters that indicate his dismay with life on the lecture circuit. "Mark Twain on the Platform" (*The Critic* [April 1896], 286) contains an excellent description of Twain in performance. *Revived Remarks on Mark Twain by George Ade*, edited by George Hiram Brownell, (Chicago: Privately Printed, 1936) also provides a contemporary's view of Twain's performances. *Critical Essays on Mark Twain*, 1867-1910, edited by Louis J. Budd, (Boston, Mass.: G. K. Hall & Co., 1982), is a collection of articles written about Twain's lectures by his contemporaries. Budd's introduction provides a particularly informative summary of Twain's speaking career.

Some journal articles concern specific speeches. D. M. McKeithan's "The Occasion of Mark Twain's Speech 'On Foreign Critics,'" (*Philological Quarterly* XXVII [July 1948], 276-279) is particularly pertinent to understanding the rhetorical situation that Twain addressed in this well-organized rebuttal. Henry Nash Smith's "That Hideous Mistake of Poor Clemens's," (*Harvard Library Bulletin* 9 [Spring 1955], 145-180) describes in great detail the occasion of Twain's "great fiasco," his speech at Whittier's birthday celebration. DeLancy Ferguson's, "Mark Twain's Last Curtain Speeches" (*South Atlantic Quarterly* XLII [1943], 262-269), presents Twain's responses on the opening nights of two of his rather unsuccessful attempts at playwriting—*The Gilded Age* and *Ah Sin*.

Several articles focus on the connection between Twain's platform performances and the development of his public image. Louis J. Budd's article "Hiding Out in Public: Mark Twain as a Speaker," (*Studies in American Fiction* 13 [Autumn 1986], 129-141) is an excellent critical essay on Twain's style of oratory and its effect on the development of his public image. Budd contends: "In his best speeches . . . Clemens and Twain merge and a third figure emerges, neither simply private nor public, neither a flesh and blood person or a literary persona but a unique, engaging, vivid, and intriguing presence" (p. 139). Budd offers a very thorough exploration of the development and impact of Twain's ethos in his book *Our Mark Twain: The*

Making of His Public Personality (Philadelphia: University of Pennsylvania Press, 1983). This excellent work recognizes the significant contribution made by Twain's platform performances to the man celebrated as the Representative American. Another essay about the contribution of Twain's performances to his public personality is "A Talent for Posturing," found in Sara BeSaussure Davis and Philip D. Beidler's anthology, *The Mythologizing of Mark Twain* (University of Alabama Press, 1984). In "The Importance of Mark Twain," (*American Quarterly* 37 [Spring 1986], 30-49), Alan Gribben credits Twain's platform experience for the development of his oral style of writing and his emergence as a mythic figure.

Other articles discuss Twain's platform experience with emphasis on his performing technique: Kraid Ashbaugh's "Mark Twain As a Public Speaker" (*Western Journal of Speech Communication* XIV [January 1950], 10-14) gives an overview of Twain's experience. Charles R. Duke's "Mark Twain: Speaker at Large," (*The English Record* [Spring 1974], 43-52) presents a biographical perspective of Twain's platform career. E. James Lennon's "Mark Twain Abroad," (*Quarterly Journal of Speech* XXXIX [April 1953], 197-200) discusses the pleasant reaction of audiences to Twain's apparent spontaneous style during his world tour of 1895-1896.

Some sources that are not directly concerned with Twain's platform career but include useful information about his public speaking should be consulted. For example, Henry Nash Smith's discussion of Twain's point of view as "a vernacular perspective" in *Mark Twain: The Development of a Writer* (Cambridge, Mass.: The Belknap Press of Harvard University Press, 1962) helps to understand the influence Twain had over his lecture audiences. Maxwell Geismar's *Mark Twain: An American Prophet* (Boston: Houghton Mifflin Company, 1970) contains a complete chapter, "Postmortem Ebullience," on Twain's speeches. Howard G. Baetzhold's *Mark Twain and John Bull: The British Connection* (Bloomington: Indiana University Press, 1970) reviews Twain's speaking in England, particularly his reception by English audiences.

Three articles that focus on the important contribution Twain made to the development of the American national spirit are also important to this study. Charles Miner Thompson's article, "Mark Twain as an Interpreter of American Character" (*Atlantic Monthly* 79 [April 1897], 443-450) is an acknowledgement of the contributions made by Twain to American society. Charles Vale's article "Mark Twain as an Orator" (*The Forum* 44, [July 1910], 1-13) written after Twain's death on April 21, 1910, is particularly relevant to this study. Vale describes Twain as a great orator and as the embodiment of the American national character. Arthur G. Pettit's "Mark Twain and His Times: A Bicentennial Appreciation "(*South Atlantic Quarterly* [Spring 1977], 133-146) reviews Twain's life and accomplishments and relates him to the present, referring to him as "our most 'contemporary' historical figure: No famous figure of our past—certainly no famous figure who rests outside the pantheon of the presidents—speaks more forcefully and personally to the sins and virtues, the triumphs and debacles of our own time." (p. 134).

BIOGRAPHICAL SOURCES

Although criticized for some factual misrepresentation, Alfred Bigelow Paine's three-volume official biography *Mark Twain: A Biography* (New York: Harper and Brothers Publishers, 1912) remains an important source for understanding the man. Its contents come from Paine's personal observation, information from Twain's acquaintances, and documentation provided by Twain and his family and friends. Archibald Henderson's *Mark Twain* (New York: F.A. Stokes, 1910) provides the reader with a thorough view of Twain's life and art, including his platform art, from the view of a contemporary. Mary Austin Baldwin's edited version of William Dean Howells's *My Mark Twain: Reminiscences and Criticisms* (Baton Rouge: Louisiana State University Press, 1967) concerns Howells' recollections of his friendship with Mark Twain. Most pertinent to this study is Howell's evaluation of Twain's platform talent. Justin Kaplan's acclaimed *Mr. Clemens and Mark Twain: A Biography* (New York: Simon and Shuster, 1966) provides the reader with a psychological interpretation of Twain's personality. Arthur L. Scott's *Mark Twain at Large* (Chicago: Henry Regnery Company, 1969) details Twain's travels and how he became an Ambassador-at-Large. Edward Wagenknecht's *Mark Twain: The Man and His Work* (Norman: University of Oklahoma Press, 1961) offers a more objective review of the man and his life. The reader may also be interested in *Mark Twain in Elmira*, edited by Robert D. Jerome and Herbert A. Wisbey, Jr. (Elmira, NY: Mark Twain Society, 1977). This book deals with Twain's stay in his wife's hometown. Mark Twain and his family are buried here. Three journals devoted exclusively to articles about Twain are *The Twainian*, published bi-monthly by the Mark Twain Research Foundation, Perry, Missouri; the *Mark Twain Society Bulletin*, edited by Robert D. Jerome and Herbert A. Wisbey, Jr., Elmira, New York; the *Mark Twain Journal*, published twice yearly and edited by Thomas A. Tenney, Charleston, South Carolina.

HISTORICAL ACCOUNTS

Two volumes vital to understanding the American national character are Daniel Boorstin's *The Americans: The National Experience* (New York: Random House, 1966) and Henry Steele Commager's *The American Mind:*

An Interpretation of American Thought and Character Since the 1880's (New Haven: Yale University Press, 1950). The first chapter in Commager's book, "The Nineteenth-Century American" is particularly pertinent to the understanding of Twain's oratory.

Two sources that will help the reader understand that Twain was a product of his environment are Frederick Jackson Turner's "The Significance of the Frontier in American History," (*American Historical Association Annual Report for 1893*, 199-227) and Bernard DeVoto's *Mark Twain's America* (Boston: Little, Brown and Company, 1932). Turner contends that the frontier "this expansion westward with its new opportunities, its continuous touch with the simplicity of primitive society" (p. 200) created the forces that developed the American character, the growth of nationalism, and the promotion of democratic ideals in America and Europe. DeVoto's book presents a somewhat romantic description of Twain's frontier background. DeVoto wrote to reply to Van Wyck Brooks' criticism of Twain's environment as an impediment to the development of his art in Brooks' *The Ordeal of Mark Twain* (New York: E.P. Dutton & Co., 1920).

Two other books offer insight into the total picture of American culture in the nineteenth century, providing the reader with a greater understanding of the rhetorical situations Twain addressed. Daniel Walker Howe's *Victorian America* (Philadelphia: University of Pennsylvania Press, 1976) describes the development and characteristics of the dominant culture, noting that Americans were more Victorian than the English. Most pertinent to this study is Howe's discussion of the conflict between this culture and changing American society.

Three books present historical accounts of the development of public speech in nineteenth-century America. Barnet Baskerville's *The People's Voice: The Orator in American Society* (Lexington: The University Press of Kentucky, 1979) traces the influence of the orator in American society from the revolutionary period, when the orator was regarded as a hero, to contemporary times, referred to as "the decline of eloquence." The author presents a very informative assessment of the four decades in which Twain was a popular orator. Kenneth Cmiel's *Democratic Eloquence: The Fight over Popular Speech in Nineteenth-Century America* (New York: William Morrow and Co., 1990) explores the evolution of popular speech from eighteen-century society to contemporary times, what the author calls "the post-rhetorical age." A particularly pertinent chapter is the second one, which discusses the development and impact of the democratic idiom. Richard Bridgman's *The Colloquial Style in America* (New York: Oxford University Press, 1966) analyzes the development of the popular idiom in America.

Two volumes that provide a greater understanding of American humor with particular emphasis on the development of folk humor—Twain's form of humor—are Walter Blair and Hamlin Hill's *America's Humor: From Poor Richard to Doonesbury* (New York: Oxford University Press, 1978) and Walter Blair's *Horse·Sense in American Humor* (New York: Russell and Russell, 1942).

Five works by contemporaries provide an in-depth understanding of the American lecture movement and its impact on the development of the American national character. Waldo Braden's "The Lecture Movement: 1840-1860" (*Quarterly Journal of Speech* 34 [1948], 206-212) describes the beginning of the movement and its characteristics before the Civil War. Thomas Higginson's "American Audiences" (*Atlantic Monthly*) 95 [January 1905], 38-44) presents an overall description of the lecture system, particularly the types of audiences. J. G. Holland's "The Popular Lecture," (*Atlantic Monthly*, 15 [March 1865] 362-371) demonstrates that the popular lecture was "the most purely democratic of all our democratic institutions" (p. 363). Charles R. Horner's *The Life of James Redpath and the Development of the Modern Lyceum* (New York: Barse & Hopkins, 1926) and James Pond's article "Great Orators and the Lyceum," (*Cosmopolitan* 21 [July 1896], 247-256) deal with representative personalities of the lecture system. Horner's book is a biography of the manager of the Boston Lyceum, the lecture group to which Twain belonged. Pond's article consists of brief essays on the great orators of the lyceum, such as John B. Gough, Wendell Phillips, Robert G. Ingersoll, Frederick Douglass, and Susan B. Anthony.

SELECTED SOURCES FOR CRITICAL ANALYSIS

The following sources are recommended for information on the history and criticism of American public address: Brigance, William Norwood, ed., *A History and Criticism of American Public Address* I, II (New York: Russell & Russell, 1960); Hochmuth, Marie Kathryn, ed., *A History of Criticism of American Public Address* III (New York: Longmans, Green and Co., 1955); and Oliver, Robert T., *History of Public Speaking in America* (Boston: Allyn and Bacón, Inc., 1965).

The following sources are recommended for rhetorical study of Twain: Herbert A. Wilchelns' classic essay "The Literary Criticism of Oratory," in *Studies in Rhetoric and Public Speaking in Honor of James Albert Winans* (New York: Russell and Russell, 1925, reprinted 1962, 181-216) concerns the need for rhetorical criticism of public speeches. Wilchelns shows that rhetorical criticism is similar to literary criticism: "A speech, like a satire, like a comedy of manners, grows directly out of a social situation; it is a man's response to a condition in human affairs" (p. 214). Wilcheln's explains that the critical method for studying oratory considers the speaker, the speaker's work, and the speaker's times. Lloyd F. Bitzer's article "The Rhetorical Situation" (*Philosophy and Rhetoric* 1 [Winter 1968], 1-15) describes the conditions within the relationship between the speaker and audience that are necessary for rhetoric to occur. Edwin Black's "The Second Persona" (*Quarterly Journal of Speech* LVI [April 1970], 109-119) posits that rhetorical discourse will imply an auditor, a second persona after the first persona, the speaker's image, and that the association between an idiom and an ideology is more than a chance happening. Wayne C. Booth's "The Rhetorical Stance," (*College Composition and Communication* XIV [October 1963], 139-145) argues the notion that persuasion occurs when the speaker achieves a rhetorical stance, that is, when the rhetor relates ethos and message to the audience. Kenneth Burke's *A Grammar of Motives and A Rhetoric of Motives* (Cleveland: The World Publishing Co., 1962) posits that society is created and maintained through symbols and, therefore, persuasion is effected when the speaker identifies with the audience with such stylistic identifications as speech, gesture, image, and attitude. In Richard Weaver's series of essays, *Ethics of Rhetoric* (Chicago: Henry Regnery Company, 1970), he emphasizes that the order of values is the ultimate sanction of rhetoric: "The rhetorician is a preacher to us" (p. 179).

Index

About the Author

Marlene Boyd Vallin is Associate Professor of Speech Communication and American Studies at the Pennsylvania State University, Berks Campus. She has published articles on public speaking, interpersonal and group communication, and performance studies in a variety of professional journals.

Great American Orators

Richard Nixon: Rhetorical Strategist
Hal W. Bochin

Henry Ward Beecher: Peripatetic Preacher
Halford R. Ryan

Edward Everett: Unionist Orator
Ronald F. Reid

Theodore Roosevelt and the Rhetoric of Militant Decency
Robert V. Friedenberg

Patrick Henry, The Orator
David A. McCants

Anna Howard Shaw: Suffrage Orator and Social Reformer
Wil A. Linkugel and Martha Solomon

William Jennings Bryan: Orator of Small-Town America
Donald K. Springen

Robert M. La Follette, Sr.: The Voice of Conscience
Carl R. Burgchardt

Ronald Reagan: The Great Communicator
Kurt Ritter and David Henry

Clarence Darrow: The Creation of an American Myth
Richard J. Jensen

"Do Everything" Reform: The Oratory of Frances E. Willard
Richard W. Leeman

Abraham Lincoln the Orator: Penetrating the Lincoln Legend
Lois J. Einhorn